I0006639

Basics of Database Management System

Manpreet Singh Bhullar
Sumeet Kumar

Basics of Database Management System

LAP LAMBERT Academic Publishing

Imprint

Any brand names and product names mentioned in this book are subject to trademark, brand or patent protection and are trademarks or registered trademarks of their respective holders. The use of brand names, product names, common names, trade names, product descriptions etc. even without a particular marking in this work is in no way to be construed to mean that such names may be regarded as unrestricted in respect of trademark and brand protection legislation and could thus be used by anyone.

Cover image: www.ingimage.com

Publisher:
LAP LAMBERT Academic Publishing
is a trademark of
International Book Market Service Ltd., member of OmniScriptum Publishing Group
17 Meldrum Street, Beau Bassin 71504, Mauritius

ISBN: 978-3-659-53893-3

Preface

First of all we are thankful for our almighty who gives us direction and knowledge to right this book. This book is specially designed for students who want to learn about Data Base Management System. This book provides a modern, self-contained, introduction to DBMS. We designed the book to be used by both learners desiring a firm foundation to build on, and practitioners in search of critical analysis and modern implementations of the most important DBMS system. This book is written in simple English language which is easily understandable by student's who first language is not an English. This book is divided into seven chapters. First lesson's gives introduction about database and general terms and models used in DBMS and in the last two lessons we try to explain MS Access basic . Each lesson is specially designed for different topic and each topic is explained with the help of particular example.

In the last we are thank to Lambert publication and our friends for providing inspiration and moral support through the writing process. We will welcome the constructive suggestions from reader for the further improvement in this book.

Manpreet Singh Bhullar

Assistant Professor

G.S.S.D.G.S Khalsa College , Patiala-Punjab-India

Sumeet Kumar

Assistant Professor

M.M Modi College , Patiala-Punjab-India

Contents

Chapter 1 Overview of Data Base Management System

Chapter 2   DBMS Architecture

Chapter 3 ER Model

Chapter 4 Data Base Models

Chapter 5 Introduction To MS Access

Chapter 1 Overview of Data Base Management System

1.1 Introduction

Twenty first century is the century of technology and computer. In the century of technology data plays very important role. **Data is** raw facts, figures, images and sounds that have little or no meaning. They have little or no meaning because they lack a context for evaluation. The company's computer is capable of processing 10,000 customer requests an hour and The Company receives an average of 9800 customer requests an hour. Each fact, by itself, is relatively meaningless because we have little or no context within which to evaluate and make sense of it.

1.2 Information

Data are also the raw facts and figures that people and computers use to process information. Data is entered into a system, stored in the system, and processed by the system. Through information processing, people, and computers summarize and/or transform data to make it meaningful and to turn it into information. Or in other words process form of data is called information.

Basically information means processed form data that is arrangement of data in some particular order. So that we can reach at some conclusion with the help of that information.

For e.g. : ABC, DEF, GHI, JKL, 60, 70, 80, 90, 101, 102, 103, 104 etc. are daa. The above data does not tell anything. If we write the above data in the following form as

Name	Roll No.	Marks
ABC	101	60
DEP	102	80
GHI	103	70
JKL	104	90

This is known as information, because from here we can come at conclusion like who is topper, who is in last position etc.

Difference between Data and Information.

Data	Information
1. Data are raw facts and figures.	1. Information is processes of data.
2. 25 is a data.	2. Age = 25 is an information.
3. Data does not help in decision making	3. Information helps in decision decision making

Data Items - Data items are also known as fields which refers to a single unit of value. For e.g : Name, roll no, city, address, pin code etc. are data items.

Data items are of two types:

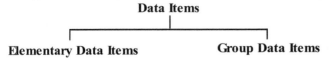

Data Items

Elementary Data Items   **Group Data Items**

Data items that cannot be further sub-divided known as elementary data items. For e.g: City, Pin code, roll no, etc.

Data items that can be further divided into sub-data items are known as group data items. For e.g.: Address is a group data item because it is divided into sub data items like house no. colony name, city, pin code etc. Name is also a group data item because it is divided into sub items like first name, middle name, last name.

1.3 Data Base

The collection of related data is known as data base or we can say that the related information when stored in an organising form is known as data base. The organisation of data is necessary because unorganised information has no meaning.

For e.g. : ABC, DEF, GHI, JKL, 101, 102, 103, 104, 60, 70, 80, 90 has no meaning. It can be organised as :

Name	Roll No.	Marks
ABC	101	60
DEF	102	70
GHI	103	80
JKl	104	90

This is known as data base.

1.4 Characteristics of data base or features of data base.

There are number of characteristics of data base. These are :

1. Sharing
2. No duplication
3. Security
4. Persistence
5. Correctness

1.   **Sharing:** It means data in one computer can be shared by different users.

2.   **No duplication:** It means there should be no repetition of data. For eg.. two students cannot have the same roll no. or registration no.

3.   **Security:** Data should be protected from authorities use that is three should be same procedures or algorithms to protect database.

4.   **Persistence:** It means database exist permanently.

5.   **Correctness:** Data should be correct with respect to real world.

1.5 Database Management System

For using data and information effectively a special software is needed which store , retrieve and manipulate data easily and efficiently and this software is called database management system. A **database management system** (**DBMS**) is a software package with computer programs that control the creation, maintenance, and the use of a database.

1.6 Advantages of DBMS's

1.   Control of data redundancy

In non-database systems (traditional computer file processing), each application program has its own files. In this case, the duplicated copies of the same data are created at many places. In DBMS, all the data of an organization is integrated into a single database. The data is recorded at only one place in the database and it is not duplicated.

2. Data consistency

By controlling the data redundancy, the data consistency is obtained. If a data item appears only once, any update to its value has to be performed only once and the updated value (new value of item) is immediately available to all users.

If the DBMS has reduced redundancy to a minimum level, the database system enforces consistency. It means that when a data item appears more than once in the database and is updated, the DBMS automatically updates each occurrence of a data item in the database.

3. Data Sharing:

In DBMS, data can be shared by authorized users of the organization. The DBA manages the data and gives rights to users to access the data. Many users can be authorized to access the same set of information simultaneously. The remote users can also share same data. Similarly, the data of same database can be shared between different application programs.

4 . Data Integration:

In DBMS, data in database is stored in tables. A single database contains multiple tables and relationships can be created between tables (or associated data entities). This makes easy to retrieve and update data.

5. Integrity Constraints:

Integrity constraints or consistency rules can be applied to database so that the correct data can be entered into database. The constraints may be applied to data item within a single record or they may be applied to relationships between records.

6. Improved security

Data is stored at one place and it is easy to provide security to data at one place . Various encryption and user access is defined in the DBMS, which provide high level of security.

7. Increased productivity

In the DBMS data is accurate and easily available to every user. No redundancy and inconsistency also improved the productivity of any organization.

8.   Improved backup and recovery services

In a computer file-based system, the user creates the backup of data regularly to protect the valuable data from damaging due to failures to the computer system or application program. It is a time consuming method, if volume of data is large. Most of the DBMSs provide the 'backup and recovery' sub-systems that automatically create the backup of data and restore data if required.

1.7 Disadvantages of DBMS

1. Cost of Hardware & Software:

A processor with high speed of data processing and memory of large size is required to run the DBMS software. It means that you have to upgrade the hardware used for file-based system. Similarly, DBMS software is also Very costly.

2. Cost of Data Conversion:

When a computer file-based system is replaced with a database system, the data stored into data file must be converted to database files. It is difficult and time consuming method to convert data of data files into database. You have to hire DBA (or database designer) and system designer along with application programmers; alternatively, you have to take the services of some software houses. So a lot of money has to be paid for developing database and related software.

3. Cost of Staff Training:

Most DBMSs are often complex systems so the training for users to use the DBMS is required. Training is required at all levels, including programming, application development, and database administration. The organization has to pay a lot of amount on the training of staff to run the DBMS.

4. Appointing Technical Staff:

The trained technical persons such as database administrator and application programmers etc are required to handle the DBMS. You have to pay handsome salaries to these persons. Therefore, the system cost increases.

5. Database Failures:

In most of the organizations, all data is integrated into a single database. If database is corrupted due to power failure or it is corrupted on the storage media, then our va

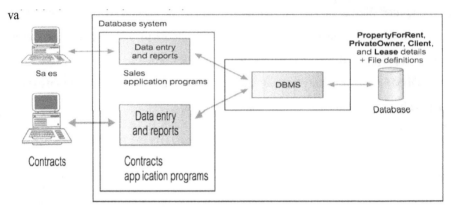

1.8 Components of DBMS

There are 4 components of DBMS :

These are :

1. Data

2. Hardware

3. Software

4. User

1. **Data:** Collection of raw facts and figures is known as data for e.g marks obtained by students.

2. **Hardware:** Physical components of computer that we can see and touch are known as hardware. The hardware is actual computer system used for keeping and accessing the data base. The hardware in database management system consists of secondary storage like hard disk, magnetic tape, compact disk (cd).

3. **Software:** A set of programs or instructions which are used to create and access data base is known as software. Basically software acts as interface between hardware and user DBMS, hides, hardware detail from user because user is known only with the data base. Examples of DBMS software's are : MS-Access, MS-Excel, FoxPro, SQL, ORACLE, etc.

4. **User:** User is that person who is able to create data base query (Query means and Store data or make the structure of data base. In other words those persons which are related to data base directly or indirectly as known as user.

1.9 **DBMS User**

2. **Application programme:**

Professional programmes who are responsible for developing application programmes are known as application programmes. Application programmes are made in any programming language like C, C++, Java, PL/SQL etc.

2. **End User :** Those user who access the data base by using simple commands are known as end user. These users have little knowledge about the programming language in which database is created. Moreover and user are only concern with their transactions and queries.

3. **Data base administrator (DBA) :** It is a person or group of person responsible for managing over all database system. The DBA has authority to allow grants to other users.

The diagram showing all the components of DBMS is:

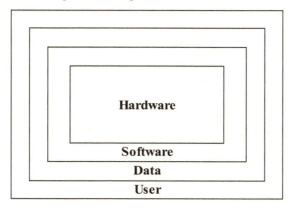

4.   Database designer: The database designers are the users who design the structure of the database. They are responsible for identifying the data to be stored in the database, the constraints for the data and you choosing appropriate structure to represent and shore the data. It communicate with all perspectives of the database users in order to understand there needs.

1.10 Instance and Schema Database changes over time as information is inserted or deleted. The collection of information store in a data base at a particular moment is known as instance. The overall design or structure of data base is called schema.

For eg: Schema to insert name, roll no, marks and percentage in C language is

       Struct Table

{

       Char Name (10) ;

       int   Roll No ;

       int   Marks ;

       int   Per ;

} ;

after making schema the table looks like

Name	Roll No.	Marks	Per

Suppose at particular instance of time, we insert data in the above table as

Name	Roll No.	Marks	Per
ABC	101	60	60
DEF	102	70	70
GHI	103	80	80
JKL	104	90	90

Now this moment at which we insert data in the above table is known as instance.

1.11 Internal schema

Internal Schema describes the physical storage structure of the database. The internal

13

schema uses a physical data model and describes the complete details of data storage and access paths for the database.

1.12 Conceptual level or Conceptual schema

It describes the structure of the whole database for a community of users. It hides the details of physical storage structures and concentrates on describing entities, data types, relationships, user operations, and constraints. Implementation data model can be used at this level.

1.13 External level or External schema

It includes a number of external schemas or user views. Each external schema describes the part of the database that a particular user is interested in and hides the rest of the database from user. Implementation data model can be used at this level.

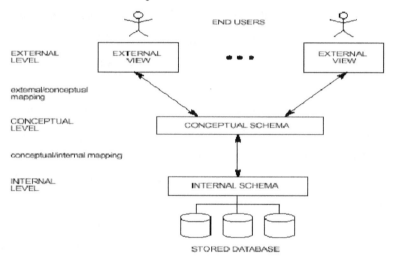

Exercise:

Q1. What is Data and Information?

Q2. Differentiate between data and information?

Q3. What is DBMS?

Q4. Write down the various advantages of DBMS?

Q5. What is Database ?

Q6. Explain various DBMS users?

Q7. What is instance and schema?

Chapter 2   DBMS Architecture

2.1 DBMS Architecture

Database Management Systems are very complex, sophisticated software applications that provide reliable management of large amounts of data. To better understand general database concepts and the structure and capabilities of a DBMS, it is useful to examine the architecture of a typical database management system.

There are two different ways to look at the architecture of a DBMS: the logical DBMS architecture and the physical DBMS architecture. The logical architecture deals with the way data is stored and presented to users, while the physical architecture is concerned with the software components that make up a DBMS.

2.2 Logical DBMS Architecture

The logical architecture describes how data in the database is perceived by users. It is not concerned with how the data is handled and processed by the DBMS, but only with how it looks. Users are shielded from the way data is stored on the underlying file system, and can manipulate the data without worrying about where it is located or how it is actually stored. This results in the database having different levels of abstraction.

The majority of commercial Database Management Systems available today are based on the ANSI/SPARC generalized DBMS architecture, as proposed by the ANSI/SPARC Study Group on Data Base Management Systems.

The ANSI/SPARC architecture divides the system into three levels of abstraction: the internal or physical level, the conceptual level, and the external or view level. The diagram below shows the logical architecture for a typical DBMS.

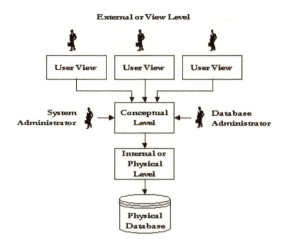

Logical DBMS Architecture

2.2.1 The Internal or Physical Level

The collection of files permanently stored on secondary storage devices is known as the physical database. The physical or internal level is the one closest to physical storage, and it provides a low-level description of the physical database, and an interface between the operating system's file system and the record structures used in higher levels of abstraction. It is at this level that record types and methods of storage are defined.

2.2.2 The Conceptual Level

The conceptual level presents a logical view of the entire database as a unified whole, which allows you to bring all the data in the database together and see it in a consistent manner. The first stage in the design of a database is to define the conceptual view, and a DBMS provides a data definition language for this purpose.

2.2.3 The External or View Level

The external or view level provides a window on the conceptual view which allows the user to see only the data of interest to them. The user can be either an application program or an end user. Any number of external schemas can be defined and they can overlap each other.

2.4 Physical DBMS Architecture

The physical architecture describes the software components used to enter and process data, and how these software components are related and interconnected .The physical DBMS architecture can be broken down into two parts: the back end and the front end.

The back end is responsible for managing the physical database and providing the

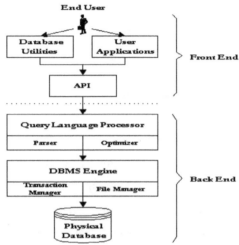

necessary support and mappings for the internal, conceptual, and external levels described earlier. Other benefits of a DBMS, such as security, integrity, and access control, are also the responsibility of the back end.

The front end is really just any application that runs on top of the DBMS. These may be applications provided by the DBMS vendor, the user, or a third party. The user interacts with the front end, and may not even be aware that the back end exists.

Both the back end and front end can be further broken down into the software components that are common to most types of DBMS. These components are examined in detail in the following sections.

2.5 Traditional File Processing Systems

File processing system was an early attempt to computerized manual file system. A file system is a method of storing and organising computer files and data they contain

file system may use storage devices such as hard disk, compact disk, floppy disk etc.

2.5.1 Characteristics of file processing system.

There are number of characteristics of file processing system.

These are :

1.   It is a group of files storing data in an organisation.

2.   Each file is independent from another file.

3.   Each file is called flat file.

4.   Each file process information for one specific function. Such as accounting or payroll.

5.   Files are designed by using programs written in program language such as cobol, C, C++ etc.

6.   These files are easy to maintain and handle.

2.6 Limitations of Traditional File Processing System

1.   **Separated and isolated data:** In traditional file processing system data is stored in different files. So for making decision, you need data from two or more separated files.

2.   **Duplication of data:** In this, when user enters information or data, lot of duplicate data can be entered by mistake which is difficult to detect. For eg : Same roll no for two or more students can be entered by mistake.

3. No data independence: In traditional file system data independence is no possible. For eg: Suppose file system is created in C language when we change the schema of file by using program, other levels are automatically changed.

4.   Less Security: In traditional file system. It is very difficult to provide security to data base.

5.   Authorization Problem: In traditional file system, we cannot give access to different users.

2.7 Data Base Administrator

A database administrator (short form DBA) is a person responsible for the design, implementation, maintenance and repair of an organization's database. One of the main reasons for using DBMS is to have a central control of both data and the

18

programs accessing those data. A person who has such control over the system is called a Database Administrator (DBA).

2.8 Responsibilities of DBA/Aims or objectives or functions of DBA :

There are number of responsibilities of DBA. These are :

1. **Schema definition :** DBA decides the storage structure of the database. DBA creates the original database schema by writing a programme in any programming language. DBA decides how data is to be represented in memory.

2. **Information Content:** Here, job of DBA is to decide exactly what information is to be store in data base. For eg: In a database of bank customers. It is the duty of DBA to decide what type of information regarding that customer is to be kept in database.

3. **Integrity constraints specification:**

Constraints mean condition that checks the data according to the condition applied in the structure of table before inserting data in the table.

Name	Address	Roll No
ABC	Delhi	101
DEF	Mumbai	102
GHI	Punjab	101

It is the job of DBA to apply the constraints on some fields. Where only unique value should be needed. For eg: consider the data base of PGDCA student having fields Name, Roll No., Registration no., Date of Birth etc. Now when we enter data in the table, then by mistake one can enter same roll no. or registration number for two or more students, which can never be possible. To avoid this situation, DBA apply constraints on these fields.

4. **Backup and Recovery:** DBA is responsible for defining procedures to recover the data base due to some miss happening. For eg : consider a bank having lac's of accounts. If due to some miss happening earthquakes or flood or fire occur, than all

the computers or records of that bank will be lost. Now, it is the responsibility of DBA to recover all the last data.

5.   **Provide Support to Users:** It is the responsibility of data base administrator to provide support to users that is to ensure that the data they need to want should be available to them.

6.   **Granting of authorisation for data access:**

It means to allow (grant) different type of operations to different users. For eg: In a college data base, data base administrator gives only vie grant two students which means students can only view their results.

7.   **Monitoring Performances and Corresponding to Change:** It is the responsibility of DBA to change database with the passage of time. For eg: Consider the database for any new grant of bank. Initially bank has few customers but with the passage of time, number of customers can be increased. So there is a need to increase the size of data base. This all is the responsibility of database administrator.

2.9   Data Base Languages

Data base languages are used to create and maintain database in a computer. There are large numbers of languages oracle, MS-Access, DBase, FoxPro, SQL etc. Database languages are of three types. These are:

1.   Data Definition language (DDL)

2.   Data Manipulation language (DML)

3.   Data Control language (DCL)

1.   Data Definition Language (DDL) :

This language is used to define the schema definition of data base. Basically, it is used to create, insert to delete or alter the data feeds. All the constraints are defined in this language. For eg: If we want to store name roll no, and marks of a students of PGDCA class, then its schema is created only in data definition language.

Name	Roll No.	Marks

20

3. **Data Manipulation Language (DML) : DML** is data manipulation language. This manipulation involves inserting data into database tables, retrieving existing data, deleting data from existing tables and modifying existing data.

Name	Roll No.	Marks
A	101	60
B	102	70
C	103	80
D	104	90

The functional capability of DML is organized in manipulation commands like SELECT, UPDATE, INSERT INTO and DELETE FROM, as described below:

SELECT: This command is used to retrieve rows from a table. The select syntax is SELECT [column name(s)] from [table name] where [conditions]. Select is the most widely used DML command in SQL.

UPDATE: This command modifies data of one or more records. An update command syntax is UPDATE table name SET column name = value where [condition].

INSERT: This command adds one or more records to a database table. The insert command syntax is INSERT INTO table name [column(s)] VALUES [value(s)].

DELETE: This command removes one or more records from a table according to specified conditions. Delete command syntax is DELETE FROM table name where [condition].

3. **Data Control Language:** This language is used to control the database. Basically, data control language is used to give authorisation and type of authority to different persons. It is also known as DCL. One cannot create or delete data base schema using data control language. Neither we can insert or delete data using data control language. It provides different types of authorities like :

- read only
- write only
- alter only
- read and write

- view all etc.

2.10.Key

A key is a single or combination of multiple fields. Its purpose is to access or retrieve data rows from table according to the requirement. The keys are defined in tables to access or sequence the stored data quickly and smoothly. They are also used to create links between different tables.

- **Candidate key** - A candidate key is a field or combination of fields that can act as a primary key field for that table to uniquely identify each record in that table.

- **Compound key** - compound key (also called a composite key or concatenated key) is a key that consists of 2 or more attributes.

- **Primary key** - a primary key is a value that can be used to identify a unique row in a table. Attributes are associated with it. Examples of primary keys are Social Security numbers (associated to a specific person) or ISBNs (associated to a specific book). In the relational model of data, a primary key is a candidate key chosen as the main method of uniquely identifying a tuple in a relation.

- **Super key** - A super key is defined in the relational model as a set of attributes of a relation variable (rear) for which it holds that in all relations assigned to that variable there are no two distinct tuples (rows) that have the same values for the attributes in this set. Equivalently a super key can also be defined as a set of attributes of a relation upon which all attributes of the relation are functionally dependent.

- **Foreign key** - a foreign key (FK) is a field or group of fields in a database record that points to a key field or group of fields forming a key of another database record in some (usually different) table. Usually a foreign key in one table refers to the primary key (PK) of another table. This way references can be made to link information together and it is an essential part of database normalization.

- **Alternate key** - An alternate key is any candidate key which is not selected to be the primary key

2.11 Data independence

Data independence is the type of data transparency that matters for a centralized DBMS. It refers to the immunity of user applications to make changes in the definition and organization of data.

Physical data independence deals with hiding the details of the storage structure from user applications. The application should not be involved with these issues, since there is no difference in the operation carried out against the data.

The data independence and operation independence together gives the feature of data abstraction. There are two levels of data independence.

2.11.1 Data Independence Types

Data independence has two types:

1. Physical Independence and

2. Logical Independence.

With knowledge about the three-scheme architecture the term data independence can be explained as follows: Each higher level of the data architecture is immune to changes of the next lower level of the architecture.

2.11.2 Physical Independence: The logical scheme stays unchanged even though the storage space or type of some data is changed for reasons of optimization or reorganization. The ability to change the physical schema without changing the logical schema is called as Physical Data Independence.

2.11.3 Logical Independence: The external scheme may stay unchanged for most changes of the logical scheme. This is especially desirable as the application software does not need to be modified or newly translated. The ability to change the logical schema without changing the external schema or application programs is called as Logical Data Independence.

Exercise:

Q1. Differentiate between Traditional File system and DBMS?

Q2. Explain DBMS architecture?

Q3. What is internal and external schema?

Q4. What is DDL, DML and DCL?

Q5. Who is DBA?

Q6. Explain the responsibilities of DBA?

Q7. Explain different type of keys in DBMS?

Chapter 3 ER Model

3.1 Introduction

The Entity - Relationship Model (E-R Model) is a high-level conceptual data model developed by Chen in 1976 to facilitate database design. Conceptual Modeling is an important phase in designing a successful database for any organization. A conceptual data model is a set of concepts that describe the structure of a database and associated retrieval and updating transactions on the database. A high level model is chosen so that all the technical aspects are also covered.

The E-R data model grew out of the exercise of using commercially available DBMS's to model the database. The E-R model is the generalization of the earlier available commercial models like the Hierarchical and the Network Model. It also allows the representation of the various constraints as well as their relationships.

So to sum up, the Entity-Relationship (E-R) Model is based on a view of a real world that consists of set of objects called entities and relationships among entity sets which are basically a group of similar objects. The relationships between entity sets is represented by a named E-R relationship and is of 1:1, 1: N or M: N type which tells the mapping from one entity set to another.

The E-R model is shown diagrammatically using Entity-Relationship (E-R) diagrams which represent the elements of the conceptual model that show the meanings and the relationships between those elements independent of any particular DBMS and implementation details.

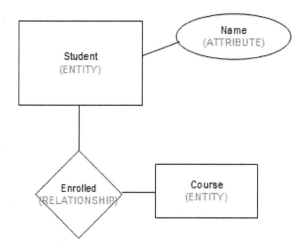

The E-R Model: The enterprise is viewed as set of

- Entities
- Relationships among entities

Symbols used in E-R Diagram

- Entity – rectangle
- Attribute – oval
- Relationship – diamond
- Link - line

3.2 Features of the E-R Model:

1. The E-R diagram used for representing E-R Model can be easily converted into Relations (tables) in Relational Model.

2. The E-R Model is used for the purpose of good database design by the database developer so to use that data model in various DBMS.

3. It is helpful as a problem decomposition tool as it shows the entities and the relationship between those entities.

4. It is inherently an iterative process. On later modifications, the entities can be inserted into this model.

5. It is very simple and easy to understand by various types of users and designers

because specific standards are used for their representation

3.3 Disadvantages of E-R Data Model

Following are disadvantages of an E-R Model:

• No industry standard for notation: There is no industry standard notation for developing an E-R diagram.

• Popular for high-level design: The E-R data model is especially popular for high level.

3.4 Record Tuple or Row

A collection of named data elements that should reflect some facts about a real world entity . Example -- "My record showing I teach this class"

RBOTTING   CS372

A Record is also called a row because it is displayed as a row in a table of similar records.

Records are also called Tuples because of the underlying discrete mathematical model of an "n-tuple". In mathematics (1,2,3) is a 3-tuple and (3,4,5,6) is a 4-tuple and so a tuple is a list of data items.

Records are also called " Logical Data Groups " because a record is a collection of data elements that go together.

3.5 Entity

An entity is a thing or object in real world which can exist and have some properties. An entity can be distinguishable from other objects. For e.g. A person is an entity, the possible properties of attributes of a person can be his name, social security number, date of birth etc. Similarly loan i an entity whose attributes are loan number, amount of issue, date of issue, amount, rate interest etc. An entity may be concrete such as student's persons etc. .

3.6 Entity Set

An entity set is a collection of entities same type that can share the same properties or attributes. The set of all persons who are customers a particular bank are defined as customer entity set. For eg :

Name	Social Security No.	A/C No.	City
ABC	101-C-97	9162	Patiala
DEF	102-D-97	8315	Sangrur
GHI	104-E-95	8112	Patiala
JKL	108-F-94	8925	Chandigarh
MNO	106-C-98	9176	Patiala

Customer Entity set

The example of abstract entity set loan is shown below which has two attributes loan no. and amount.

Loan No.	Amount
L-101	1 Lac
L-102	2 Lac
L-103	15 Lac
L-104	3 Lac
L-105	2 Lac

Loan entity set

3.7 Strong and Weak Entity

Based on the concept of foreign key, there may arise a situation when we have to relate an entity having a primary key of its own and an entity not having a primary key of its own. In such a case, the entity having its own primary key is called a strong entity and the entity not having its own primary key is called a weak entity. Whenever we need to relate a strong and a weak entity together, the ERD would change just a little. Say, for example, we have a statement "A Student lives in a Home." STUDENT is obviously a strong entity having a primary key Roll. But HOME may not have a unique primary key, as its only attribute Address may be shared by many homes (what if it is a housing estate?). HOME is a weak entity in this case.

The ERD of this statement would be like the following

As you can see, the weak entity itself and the relationship linking a strong and weak entity must

Weak Entity Set	**Strong Entity Set**
1. It does not have sufficient attributes to form a primary key.	1. It always has an attribute (s) to form a primary key.
2. Member of weak entity set is known as subordinate entity.	2. Dominant entity set.
4. Double rectangle	4. Single rectangle. have double border.

3.8 Attributes

Property of entity is known as attributes for eg : Attribute of any entity set say customer can be name social security no., address, date of birth etc. Attributes are of three types :

1. Simple attribute
2. Composite attribute
3. Null attribute
4. Derived attribute

1. Simple attribute:

Those attribute which cannot be sub-divide are known as simple attribute. Examples of simple attribute are account no, social security no, city, pin code etc.

2. Composite Attribute

Those attributes which can be further divided into sub attributes are known as composite attribute. For e.g. Name is a composite attribute because it is divided into sub attributes like first name, middle name, last name. Another example of composite attribute is date of birth because it is divided into sub attributes like day, month and year. Address is also a composite attribute because it is divided into sub attributes like house no., colony name city, pin code etc.

3.   Null Attribute :

Sometimes attributes can't have any value. For this, it is mandatory to that cell. This type of attribute is called null attribute.

4   Derived Attribute

Attribute whose values are generated from other attributes

E.g. AcctBalance = TotalCredit – TotalDebit

3.9 Relationship

A relationship is an association between several entities. For eg: consider the two entity set as show below where we define relationship borrower to denote association between customer and loan entity set.

Name	Social Security No.		A/C	Loan No.	Amount
ABC	101-C-97	A-I	L-I	1 Lac	
EFD	109-C-97	A-II	L-II	2 Lac	
DEC	101-C-98	A-III	L-III	3 Lac	
FHI	102-C-99	A-IV	L-IV	3 Lac	

3.10 Mapping Cardinalities

Mapping cardinalities express the no. of entities to which another entity of entity set can be associated by some relationship. There are of mapping cardinalities. These are:

1.   One to One

2.   One to Many

3.   Many to One

4.   Many to Many

One to One

An entity in an entity set 'A' is associated at most one entity of entity set 'B' and an entity of entity set 'B' is associated with almost one entity is entity set 'A' is known as one to one mapping.

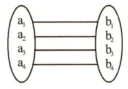

For eg: Each student has one roll no. and one roll no. is allocated to only one student. This type of association is called one to one mapping.

One to Many mapping

An entity in entities set A is associated with many entities of entity set B and many entities of entity set B are link with only one entity of entity set A is known as one to many mapping.

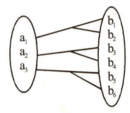

For eg: Consider two entity set class and students. Class entity set contains no. of classes and student entity set contain name of students. Now in a particular say PGDCA there can be no. of students. Similar in BCA class there can be no. of students. And on the other side no. of students may be in one class. This type of association is called one to many mapping. For eg:

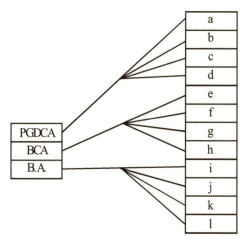

3. **Many to one :** If many entities of entity set A are associated with one entity of entity set B and one entity set B is associated with many entitles of set A is known as many to one relationship or mapping cardinalities.

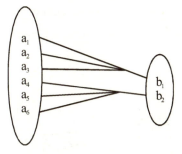

For eg: Consider entity set student an entity set class. Studene entity set contains name of different students and class entity set contains name of classes. Now, many students of entity set student are admitted in one class of entity set class. An one class of entity set class contains many students of entity set student. This type of mapping is known as many to one mapping.

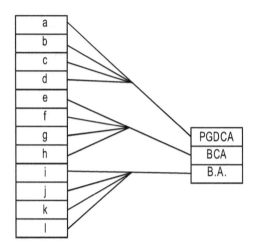

Many to Many

In many to many mapping cardinality, many entities of entity set A are related to many entities of entity set B and many entities of entity set B are related to many entities of entity set A.

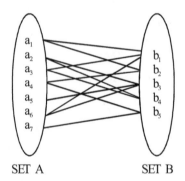

SET A   SET B

For eg: Consider two entity sets student and subject. Student entity set contain name of students and subject entity set contain name of subjects. Now many student have taken many subjects and many subjects are taken by many students. This type of mapping is known as many to many mapping.

3.11 ER Diagram

Entity relationship diagram is a graphical representation of the entities and the relationships between them. Entity relationship diagrams are a useful medium to achieve a common understanding of data among users and application developers.

The ERD tool provides all the usual features of a data modeling tool and additionally provides reverse engineering and code generation facilities. This allows a user to quickly create a database system on a number of different target platforms without the need to write any Data Definition Language (DDL) type code.

3.11.1 ER diagram Symbols

In ER diagram we use rectangles , ellipse , diamond and some other symbols which are explained below.

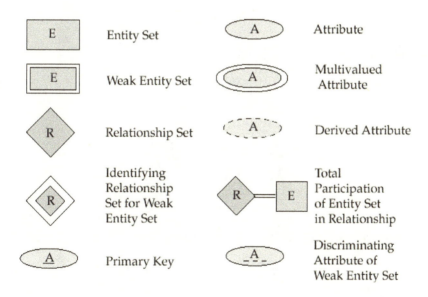

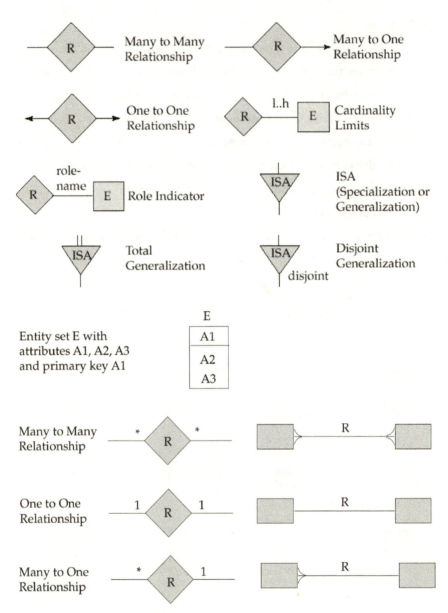

3.12 How to Prepare an ERD

Step1

Let us take a very simple example and we try to reach a fully organized database from it. Let us look at the following simple statement:

A   boy   eats   an   ice   cream.

This is a description of a real word activity, and we may consider the above statement as a written document (very short, of course).

Step2

Now we have to prepare the ERD. Before doing that we have to process the statement a little. We can see that the sentence contains a subject (*boy*), an object (*ice cream*) and a verb (*eats*) that defines the relationship between the subject and the object. Consider the nouns as entities (*boy* and *ice cream*) and the verb (*eats*) as a relationship. To plot them in the diagram, put the nouns within rectangles and the relationship within a diamond. Also, show the relationship with a directed arrow, starting from the subject entity (*boy*) towards the object entity (*ice cream*).

Well, fine. Up to this point the ERD shows how *boy* and *ice cream* are related. Now, every boy must have a name, address, phone number etc. and every ice cream has a manufacturer, flavor, price etc. Without these the diagram is not complete. These items which we mentioned here are known as attributes, and they must be incorporated in the ERD as connected ovals.

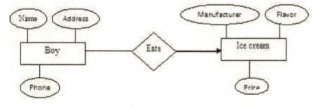

But can only entities have attributes? Certainly not. If we want then the relationship must have their attributes too. These attribute do not inform anything more either about the*boy* or the *ice cream*, but they provide additional information about the relationships between the *boy* and the *ice cream*.

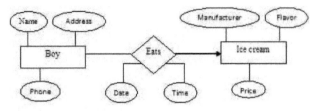

Step3

We are almost complete now. If you look carefully, we now have defined structures for at least three tables like the following:

Boy

Name	Address	Phone

Ice Cream

Manufacturer	Flavor	Price

Eats

Date	Time

However, this is still not a working database, because by definition, database should be "collection of related tables." To make them connected, the tables must have some common attributes. If we chose the attribute Name of the **Boy** table to play the role of the common attribute, then the revised structure of the above tables become something like the following.

Boy

Name	Address	Phone

Ice Cream

Manufacturer	Flavor	Price	Name

Eats

Date	Time	Name

This is as complete as it can be. We now have information about the boy, about the ice cream he has eaten and about the date and time when the eating was done.

3.13 Generalization

Generalization is a bottom-up approach in which two lower level entities combine to form a higher level entity. In generalization, the higher level entity can also combine with other lower level entity to make further higher level entity.

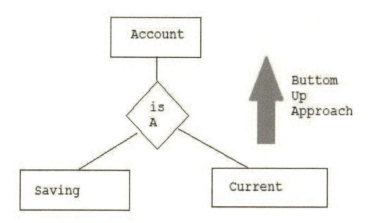

3.14 Specialization

Specialization is opposite to Generalization. It is a top-down approach in which one higher level entity can be broken down into two lower level entity. In specialization, some higher level entities may not have lower-level entity sets at all.

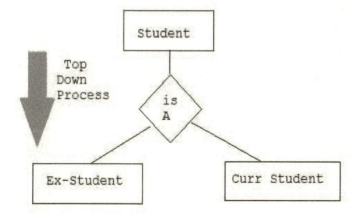

3.15 Aggregation

Aggregation is a process when relation between two entity is treated as a single entity. Here the relation between Canter and Course, is acting as an Entity in relation with Visitor.

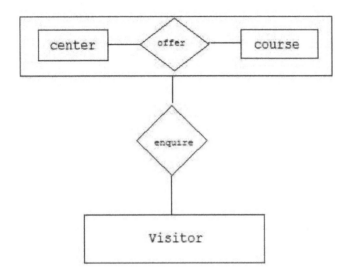

Exercise:

Q1. What is Entity and Attribute?

Q2. Explain different type of attributes?

Q3. What is ER model?

Q4. What is ER diagram?

Q5. Differentiate between generalization and specialization?

Q6. Explain various symbols used in ER diagram?

Chapter 4 Data Base Models

4.1 Data Models

A **database model** is a type of data model that determines the logical structure of a database and fundamentally determines in which manner data can be stored, organized, and manipulated. The optimal structure depends on the natural organization of the application's data, and on the application's requirements, which include transaction rate (speed), reliability, maintainability, scalability, and cost. Most database management systems are built around one particular data model, although it is possible for products to offer support for more than one model. Data models are divided into three main groups which are further divide into sub models.

1.   Object Based Data Model
2.   Physical Data Model
3.   Record Based Data Model

4.2 Object Based Logical Model

The object based models use the concepts of entities or objects and relationships among them rather than the implementation based concepts such as records used in the record based models Object based logical models provide flexible structuring capabilities and allow data constraints tobe specified explicitly. The other models that come under Object Based Logical Model are given below.

1.   Entity-relationship model.
2.   Object-oriented model.
3.   Binary model.
4.   Semantic data model.
5.   Functional data model.

4.3 Physical Data Model

Physical data models describe how data is stored in the computer, representing information such as record structures, record ordering, and access paths. There are not as many physical data models as logical data models, the most common one being the Unifying Model.

4.4 Record Based Model

Record based models are so named because the database is structured in fixed format records of several types. Each record type defines a fixed number of fields or attributes and each field is usually of a fixed length. The use of fixed length records simplifies the physical level implementation of the database. The relational model has established itself as the primary data model for commercial data processing applications. The various Record based data models are:

1. Hierarchical Model
2. Network Model
3. Relational Model

4.5 Hierarchical Model

In this model, data is stored in the form of a tree. The data is represented by parent child relationship. Each tree contains a single root record and one or more Subordinate records. For example, each batch is root and students of the batch will be subordinates.

This model supports only one-to-many relationship between entities. For example, an organization might store information about an employee, such as name, employee number, department, salary. The organization might also store information about an employee's children, such as name and date of birth. The employee and children data forms a hierarchy, where the employee data represents the parent segment and the children data represents the child segment. If an employee has three children, then there would be three child segments associated with one employee segment. In a hierarchical database the parent-child relationship is one to many. This restricts a child segment to having only one parent segment. Hierarchical DBMSs were popular from the late 1960s, with the introduction of IBM's Information Management System (IMS) DBMS, through the 1970s.

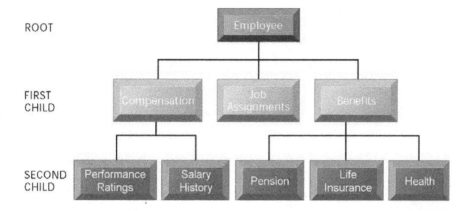

The hierarchical database model looks like an organizational chart or a family tree. It has a single root segment (Employee) connected to lower level segments (Compensation, Job Assignments, and Benefits). Each subordinate segment, in turn, may connect to other subordinate segments. Here, Compensation connects to Performance Ratings and Salary History. Benefits connects to Pension, Life Insurance, and Health. Each subordinate segments the child of the segment directly above it.

4.5.1 Properties of a Hierarchical Model

1. One record type, called the root of the hierarchical schema, does not participate as a child record type in any PCR type.

2. Every record type except the root participants as a child record type in exactly one PCR type.

3. A record type can participate as parent record type in any number (zero or more) of PCR types.

4. A record type that does not participate as parent record type in any PCR is called a leaf of the hierarchical schema.

5. If a record type participate as parent in more than one PCR type, then its child record types are ordered. The order is displayed, by convention, from   left to right in a hierarchical diagram.

4.5.2 AdvantagesHierarchical Model

The model allows easy addition and deletion of new information. Data at the top of the Hierarchy is very fast to access. It was very easy to work with the model because it worked well with linear type data storage such as tapes. The model relates very well to natural hierarchies such as assembly plants and employee organization in corporations. It relates well to anything that works through a one to many relationship. For example; there is a president with many managers below them, and those managers have many employees below them, but each employee has only one manager.

4.5.3 DisadvantagesHierarchical Model

This model has many issues that hold it back now that we require more sophisticated relationships. It requires data to be repetitively stored in many different entities. The database can be very slow when searching for information on the lower entities. We no longer use linear data storage mediums such as tapes so that advantage is null. Searching for data requires the DBMS to run through the entire model from top to bottom until the required information is found, making queries very slow. Can only model one to many relationships, many to many relationships are not supported. Clever manipulation of the model are required to make many to may relationships. For example; what if a professor teaches classes, and is also a graduate student.

4.6 Network Model

The Network model replaces the hierarchical tree with a graph thus allowing more general connections among the nodes. The main difference of the network model from the hierarchical model, is its ability to handle many to many (N:N) relations. In other words, it allows a record to have more than one parent. Suppose an employee works for two departments. The strict hierarchical arrangement is not possible here and the tree becomes a more generalized graph - a network. The network model was evolved to specifically handle non-hierarchical relationships. As shown below data can belong to more than one parent. Note that there are lateral connections as well as top-down connections. A network structure thus allows 1:1 (one: one), 1: M (one: many), M: M (many: many) relationships among entities. In network database terminology, a relationship is a set. Each set is made up of at least two types of records: an owner record (equivalent to parent in the hierarchical model) and a member record (similar to the child record in the hierarchical model).

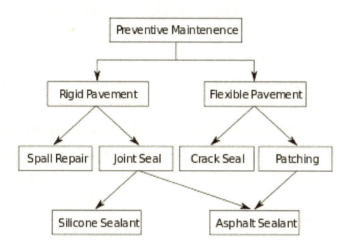

In the network model, entities are organized in a graph, in which some entities can be accessed through several path

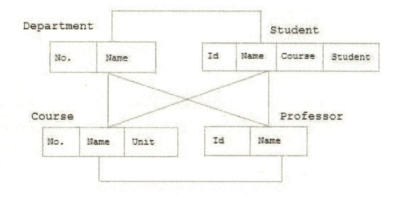

4.6.1 ADVANTAGES of Network Model

Simplicity

The network model is conceptually simple and easy to design.

Ability to handle more relationship types

The network model can handle the one-to-many and many-to-many relationships.

44

Ease of data access

In the network database terminology, a relationship is a set. Each set comprises of two types of record. - an owner record and a member record, In a network model an application can access an owner record and all the member records within a set.

Data Integrity

In a network model, no member can exist without an owner. A user must therefore first define the owner record and then the member record. This ensures the integrity.

Data Independence

The network model draws a clear line of demarcation between programs and the complex physical storage details. The application programs work independently of the data. Any changes made in the data characteristics do not affect the application program.

4.6.2 DISADVANTAGES of Network Model

System complexity

In a network model, data are accessed one record at a time. This makes it essential for the database designers, administrators, and programmers to be familiar with the internal data structures to gain access to the data. Therefore, a user friendly database management system cannot be created using the network model

Lack of Structural independence.

Making structural modifications to the database is very difficult in the network database model as the data access method is navigational. Any changes made to the database structure require the application programs to be modified before they can access data. Though the network model achieves data independence, it still fails to achieve structural independence.

4.7 Relational Model

The relational model for database management is a mathematical model for describing the structure of data. It is a database model based on first-order predicate logic, first formulated and proposed in 1969 by Edgar F. Codd., In the relational model of a database, all data is represented in terms of tuples, grouped into relations. A database organized in terms of the relational model is a relational database.

The Three Parts of the Relational Model

The relational model can be considered as having three parts and these are covered in sequence below:

1. Structural: defines the core of the data and the relationships involved. The model structure is described in terms of relations, tuples, attributes and domains.

2. Manipulative: defines how the data in the model will beaccessed and manipulated. This concerns how relations in the model will be manipulated to produce other relations, which in turn provide the answer to some question posed by a user of the data. The manipulation is achieved though relational algebra or relational calculus.

3. Constraints: defines limits on the model. The constraints determine validranges and values of data to be included in the model.

4.7.1 Advantages of the relational model

- The data model and access to it is simple to understand and use, even for those who are not.
- experienced programmers.
- The model of data represented in tables is very simple.
- Access to data via the model does not require navigation (roughly, following pointers), as do the CODASYL and network models.
- It admits a simple (in principle), declarative query language.
- There are straightforward database design procedures.
- Efficient implementation techniques are well known and widely used.
- Standards exist both for query languages (SQL)and for interfaces via programming languages(embedded SQL and ODBC/CLI).

4.7.2 Limitations of the Relational Model

1. Object identity

In entity-relationship modeling, explicit object types, such as Employee, Department, Project, etc, are specified. In the relational model, these may survive only as names of relations. In the relational model, entities have no independent identification or existence. Objects can only be identified and accessed indirectly via the identification of those attributes which characterize them.

2. Explicit relationships

In entity-relationship modeling, explicit entities and relationships were specified. In the relational model, the identities of relationships have no explicit representation. Relationships must be recovered by executing query operations on the database. These relationships must be known to the user from information not contained in the relational representation. There is a hidden semantics in the relational model.

3 Hardware overheads

relational database systems hide the implementation complexities and the physical data storage details from the user. For doing this, the relational database system need more powerful hardware computers and data storage devices.

4 Ease of design can lead to bad design

the relational database is easy to design and use. The user needs not to know the complexities of the data storage. This ease of design and use can lead to the development and implementation of the very poorly designed database management system.

4.8 Comparative Study of Hierarchical Model, Network Model and Relational Model.

Characteristic	Hierarchical model	Network model	Relational model
Relationship	One to many or one to one relationships	Allowed the network model to support many to many relationships	One to One, One to many, Many to many relationships

In hierarchical model only one-to-many or one-to-one relationships can be exist. But in network data model makes it possible to map many to many relationships In relational each record can have multiple parents and multiple child records. In effect, it supports many to many relationships

Data structure	Based on parent child relationship	A record can have many parents as well as many children.	Based on relational data structures

In hierarchical model relationship based in terms of parent child. So a child may only have one parent but a parent can have multiple children. But in network data model a record can have many parents as well as many children. Relational data model is based on relational data structures

Data manipulation	Does not provide an independent standalone query interface	CODASYL (Conference on Data Systems Languages)	Relational databases are what brings many sources into a common query (such as SQL)

In relational database it use powerful operations such as SQL languages or query by example are used to manipulate data stored in the database But in hierarchical data model it does not provide an independent standalone query interface while network model uses CODASYL

Data manipulation	retrieve algorithms are complex and asymmetric	Retrieve algorithms are complex and symmetric	Retrieve algorithms are simple and symmetric

In hierarchical data model and network model retrieve algorithms are complex and symmetric But in relational data model retrieve algorithms are simple and symmetric

Data integrity	Cannot insert the information of a child	Does not suffer from any insertion anomaly.	Does not suffer from any insert

	who does not have any parent.		anomaly.
In hierarchical data model we cannot insert the information of a child who does not have any parent. But in network model does not suffer from any insertion anomaly. relational model does not suffer from any insert anomaly			
Data integrity	Multiple occurrences of child records which lead to problems of inconsistency during the update operation	Free from update anomalies.	Free form update anomalies
In network model it is free from update anomalies because there is only a single occurrence for each record set. In relational model it also free form update anomalies because it removes the redundancy of data by proper designing through normalization process. But in hierarchical model there are multiple occurrences of child records. which lead to problems of inconsistency during the update operation			
Data integrity	Deletion of parent results in deletion of child records	Free from delete anomalies	Free from delete anomalies
In hierarchical model it is based on parent child relationship and deletion of parent results in deletion of child records .But in network model and in relational model it is free from deletion anomalies. Because information is stored in different tables.			

4.9 Normalization of Database

Normalization is a systematic approach of decomposing tables to eliminate data redundancy and undesirable characteristics like Insertion, Update and Deletion Anomalies. It is a two-step process that puts data into tabular form by removing duplicated data from the relation tables.

Normalization is used for mainly two purposes,

- Eliminating redundant(useless) data.

- Ensuring data dependencies make sense i.e data is logically stored.

4.9.1 Problem without Normalization

Without Normalization, it becomes difficult to handle and update the database, without facing data loss. Insertion, Updating and Deletion Anomalies are very frequent if Database is not normalized. To understand these anomalies let us take an example of Student table.

S_id	S_Name	S_Address	Subject_opted
401	Adam	Noida	Bio
402	Alex	Panipat	Maths
403	Stuart	Jammu	Maths
404	Adam	Noida	Physics

- **Updation Anamoly :** To update address of a student who occurs twice or more than twice in a table, we will have to update **S_Address** column in all the rows, else data will become inconsistent.

- **Insertion Anamoly :** Suppose for a new admission, we have a Student id(S_id), name and address of a student but if student has not opted for any subjects yet then we have to insert **NULL** there, leading to Insertion Anamoly.

- **Deletion Anamoly :** If (S_id) 401 has only one subject and temporarily he drops it, when we delete that row, entire student record will be deleted along with it.

4.9.2 Normalization Rule

Normalization rule are divided into following normal form.

1. First Normal Form
2. Second Normal Form
3. Third Normal Form
4. BCNF
5. Fifth Normal Form

4.9.3 First Normal Form (1NF)

A row of data cannot contain repeating group of data i.e each column must have a unique value. Each row of data must have a unique identifier i.e **Primary key**. For example consider a table which is not in First normal form

Student Table :

S_id	S_Name	Subject
401	Adam	Biology
401	Adam	Physics
402	Alex	Maths
403	Stuart	Maths

You can clearly see here that student name **Adam** is used twice in the table and subject **math** is also repeated. This violates the **First Normal form**. To reduce above table to **First Normal form** break the table into two different tables

New Student Table :

S_id	S_Name
401	Adam
402	Alex
403	Stuart

Subject Table :

subject_id	student_id	Subject

10	401	Biology
11	401	Physics
12	402	Math
12	403	Math

In Student table concatenation of subject_id and student_id is the **Primary key**. Now both the Student table and Subject table are normalized to first normal form

4.9.4 Second Normal Form (2NF)

A table to be normalized to **Second Normal Form** should meet all the needs of **First Normal Form** and there must not be any partial dependency of any column on primary key. It means that for a table that has concatenated primary key, each column in the table that is not part of the primary key must depend upon the entire concatenated key for its existence. If any column depends oly on one part of the concatenated key, then the table fails **Second normal form**. For example, consider a table which is not in Second normal form.

Customer Table :

customer_id	Customer_Name	Order_id	Order_name	Sale_detail
101	Adam	10	order1	sale1
101	Adam	11	order2	sale2
102	Alex	12	order3	sale3
103	Stuart	13	order4	sale4

In **Customer** table concatenation of Customer_id and Order_id is the primary key. This table is in **First Normal form** but not in **Second Normal form** because there are partial dependencies of columns on primary key. Customer_Name is only dependent on customer_id, Order_name is dependent on Order_id and there is no link between sale_detail and Customer_name.

To reduce **Customer** table to **Second Normal form** break the table into following three different tables.

Customer_Detail Table :

customer_id	Customer_Name
101	Adam
102	Alex
103	Stuart

Order_Detail Table :

Order_id	Order_Name
10	Order1
11	Order2
12	Order3
13	Order4

Sale_Detail Table :

customer_id	Order_id	Sale_detail
101	10	sale1
101	11	sale2
102	12	sale3
103	13	sale4

Now all these three table comply with **Second Normal form**.

4.9.5 Third Normal Form (3NF)

Third Normal form applies that every non-prime attribute of table must be dependent on primary key. The *transitive functional dependency* should be removed from the table. The table must be in **Second Normal form**. For example, consider a table with following fields.

Student_Detail Table :

Student_id	Student_name	DOB	Street	city	State	Zip

In this table Student_id is Primary key, but street, city and state depends upon Zip. The dependency between zip and other fields is called **transitive dependency**. Hence to apply **3NF**, we need to move the street, city and state to new table, with **Zip** as primary key.

New Student_Detail Table :

Student_id	Student_name	DOB	Zip

Address Table :

Zip	Street	city	State

The advantage of removing transtive dependency is,

- Amount of data duplication is reduced.
- Data integrity achieved.

4.9.6 Boyce-Code Normal Form (BCNF)

A relationship is said to be in BCNF if it is already in 3NF and the left hand side of every dependency is a candidate key. A relation which is in 3NF is almost always in BCNF. These could be same situation when a 3NF relation may not be in BCNF the following conditions are found true.

1. The candidate keys are composite.
2. There are more than one candidate keys in the relation.
3. There are some common attributes in the relation.

Professor Code	Department	Head of Dept.	Percent Time
P1	Physics	Ghosh	50
P1	Mathematics	Krishnan	50
P2	Chemistry	Rao	25
P2	Physics	Ghosh	75
P3	Mathematics	Krishnan	100

Consider, as an example, the above relation. It is assumed that:

1. A professor can work in more than one department

2. The percentage of the time he spends in each department is given.

3. Each department has only one Head of Department.

The relation diagram for the above relation is given as the following:

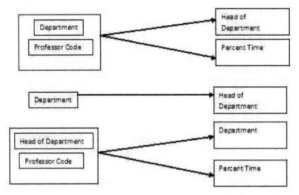

The given relation is in 3NF. Observe, however, that the names of Dept. and Head of Dept. are duplicated. Further, if Professor P2 resigns, rows 3 and 4 are deleted. We lose the information that Rao is the Head of Department of Chemistry.

The normalization of the relation is done by creating a new relation for Dept. and Head of Dept. and deleting Head of Dept. form the given relation. The normalized relations are shown in the following.

Professor Code	Department	Percent Time
P1	Physics	50
P1	Mathematics	50

P2	Chemistry	25
P2	Physics	75
P3	Mathematics	100

Department	Head of Dept.
Physics	Ghosh
Mathematics	Krishnan
Chemistry	Rao

See the dependency diagrams for these new relations.

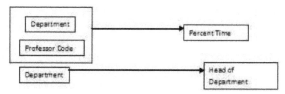

4.9.7 Fourth Normal Form (4NF)

When attributes in a relation have multi-valued dependency, further Normalization to 4NF and 5NF are required. Let us first find out what multi-valued dependency is.

A **multi-valued dependency** is a typical kind of dependency in which each and every attribute within a relation depends upon the other, yet none of them is a unique primary key.

We will illustrate this with an example. Consider a vendor supplying many items to many projects in an organization. The following are the assumptions:

1. A vendor is capable of supplying many items.
2. A project uses many items.
3. A vendor supplies to many projects.
4. An item may be supplied by many vendors.

A multi valued dependency exists here because all the attributes depend upon the other and yet none of them is a primary key having unique value.

Vendor Code	Item Code	Project No.
V1	I1	P1

V1	I2	P1
V1	I1	P3
V1	I2	P3
V2	I2	P1
V2	I3	P1
V3	I1	P2
V3	I1	P3

The given relation has a number of problems. For example:

1.   If vendor V1 has to supply to project P2, but the item is not yet decided, then a row with a blank for item code has to be introduced.

2.   The information about item I1 is stored twice for vendor V3.

Observe that the relation given is in 3NF and also in BCNF. It still has the problem mentioned above. The problem is reduced by expressing this relation as two relations in the Fourth Normal Form (4NF). A relation is in 4NF if it has no more than one independent multi valued dependency or one independent multi valued dependency with a functional dependency.

The table can be expressed as the two 4NF relations given as following. The fact that vendors are capable of supplying certain items and that they are assigned to supply for some projects in independently specified in the 4NF relation.

Vendor-Supply

Vendor Code	Item Code
V1	I1
V1	I2
V2	I2
V2	I3
V3	I1

Vendor-Project

Vendor Code	Project No.

V1	P1
V1	P3
V2	P1
V3	P2

4.9.8 Fifth Normal Form (5NF)

These relations still have a problem. While defining the 4NF we mentioned that all the attributes depend upon each other. While creating the two tables in the 4NF, although we have preserved the dependencies between Vendor Code and Item code in the first table and Vendor Code and Item code in the second table, we have lost the relationship between Item Code and Project No. If there were a primary key then this loss of dependency would not have occurred. In order to revive this relationship we must add a new table like the following. Please note that during the entire process of normalization, this is the only step where a new table is created by joining two attributes, rather than splitting them into separate tables.

Project No.	Item Code
P1	11
P1	12
P2	11
P3	11
P3	13

Exercise:

Q1. What is Data Model?

Q2. Write a short note on Hierarchical Model?

Q3. What is Relational Model?

Q4. Differentiate between Hierarchical and network model?

Q5. What is Normalization?

Q6. Differentiate between BCNF and 3rd normal form?

Q7. What is 5th normal form?

Chapter 5 Introduction To Ms Access

Microsoft Access, often abbreviated "MS Access," is a popular database application for Windows. Access allows users to create custom databases that store information in an organized structure. The program also provides a visual interface for creating custom forms, tables, and SQL queries. Data can be entered into an Access database using either visual forms or a basic spreadsheet interface. The information stored within an Access database can be browsed, searched, and accessed from other programs, including Web services.

While Access is a proprietary database management system (DBMS), it is compatible with other database programs since it supports Open Database Connectivity (ODBC). This allows data to be sent to and from other database programs, such as MS SQL, FoxPro, File maker Pro, and Oracle databases. This compatibility also enables Access to serve as the back end for a database-driven website. In fact, Microsoft FrontPage and Expression Web, as well as ASP.NET have built-in support for Access databases. For this reason, websites hosted on Microsoft Windows servers often use Access databases for generating dynamic content

5.1 HOW TO START MS ACCESS

MS- Access is a software application for managing databases. MS-Access enables you to store, retrieve, organize and analyze data stored in a database.

5.1.1 Database Objects

The most fundamental object is the table object. Table object where the data is stored in the database. There are other database objects tools that allow the user to manipulate the data held in the table.

• A query is a tool that allows the user to request specific data to be collected from the database.

• A form provides the user with an alternative interface for entering, editing and viewing data.

• A report is a tool for producing formatted printed output from the database.

• A macro is an Object that allows the database to be automated without the need for programming.

60

- A module is an Object that stores Access code written by the user.

5.2 Features of Ms-Access

In Microsoft Access, anything that can have a name is an object. In an Access Database, the main objects are tables, queries, forms, reports, data access pages, macros, and modules.

5.2.1 Database

A database is a file in which you can store data include all the other objects related to the stored data. The term database used to refer to only those files in which you save data.

When you open a database, the Database window will show you the various objects (tables, queries, forms, reports, macros and modules) that make up that database. This window acts as the control centre for the database and is the focal point for all operations involving opening, closing and creating new objects.

Objects bar

Fig 5.1

5.2.2 Table

A table is a collection of related data. Tables organise data into columns (called fields) and rows (called records). Each record relates to a single entity and each field is used to store a particular piece of information.

An object is used to store data. Each table contains information about a particular subject, such as students or books. Table contains Fields (or columns) that store different kinds of data, such as name or an address, and, Records (or rows) that collect all the information about a particular instance of the subject.

E.g. Information about a student

61

You can define a primary key (a unique value for each record) to help to retrieve your data efficiently.

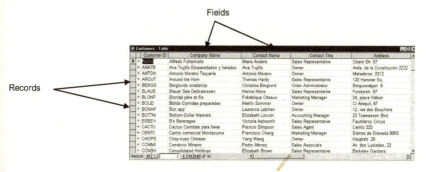

5.2.3 Query

Query in an object that provides a custom view of data from one or more tables. In Access, you can use the graphical query by example (QBE) facility or you can write SQL statements to create your queries. You can define queries to select, update, insert, or delete data. You can also define queries that create new tables from data in one or more existing tables.

5.2.4 Form

An object designed primarily for data input or display or for control; of application execution. You can use forms to customize the presentation of data that your application extracts for queries or tables. You can design a form to run a macro or a Visual Basic procedure in response to any of a number of events- for example, to run a procedure when the value of data changes.

5.2.5 Report

An object designed for formatting, calculating, printing, and summarizing selected data. You can view a report on your screen before you take print it.

5.2.6 Data Access Page

An object that includes an HTML file and supporting files to provide custom access to your data from browser such as Microsoft Internet Explorer.

5.2.7 Macro

Macro is an object that is a structured definition of one or more actions that you want Access to perform in response to a defined event. E.g you might design a macro that opens a second form in response to the selection of an item on a main form. You might have another macro that validate the content of a field whenever the value in the field changes. You can include simple conditions in macros to specify when one or more actions in the macro should be performed or skipped. You can use macros to open and execute queries, to open tables, or to print or view reports. You can also run other macros or visual Basic procedures from within a macro.

5.2.8 Module

It is an object containing custom procedures that you code using Visual Basic. Modules provide a more discrete flow of actions and allow you to trap errors something you can't do with macros. Modules can be stand-alone objects containing functions that can be called from anywhere in your application, or they can be directly associated with a form or a report to respond to events on the associated form or report.

Table stores the data that you can extract with queries and display in reports or that you can display and update in forms or data access pages. Notice that forms, reports, and data access pages can use data either directly from tables or from a filtered "view" of the data created by using queries. Queries can use Visual; Basic functions to provide customized calculations on data in your database. Access also has many built-in functions that allow you to summarize and format your data in queries.

Events on forms and reports can "trigger" either macros or Visual Basic procedures.

5.2.9 Event

Event is any change in state of an Access object. For example, you can write macros or Visual Basic procedures to respond to

• Opening a form

• Closing a form

• Entering a new row on a form

• Changing data in the current record

63

5.2.10 Control

Control is an object on a form or report that contains data. You can even design a macro or a Visual Basic procedure that responds to the user pressing individual keys on the keyboard when entering data.

5.3 WORKING WITH DATABASE AND TABLES

5.3.1 Creating a new database

When you first start Access, you see a blank work area on the left and the Home task pane on the right, as shown below.

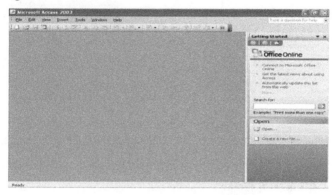

Fig-5.3

5.3.2 Using a database template to create a database

When you start Access, click **New** on the **Database** toolbar; then, in the **New File** task pane, under **Templates**, click **On my computer**.

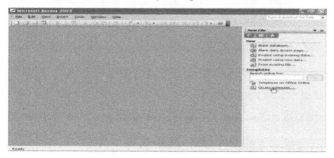

Fig-5.4

When you click on my computer, Access opens the templates dialog box. Click the databases tab of this dialog box to see a list of the 10 available templates, as shown in the following illustration.

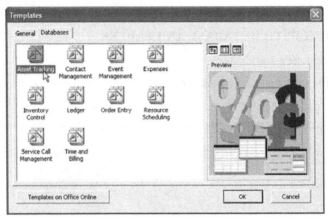

Fig 5.5

You work with all the templates in the Database Wizard in the same way. This example will show you the steps that are needed to build an Asset Tracking database. Check the list of available templates on the databases tab of the templates dialog box. When you click a template icon, Access shows a preview graphic to give you another hint about the purpose of the template. You start the Database Wizard by selecting a template and then clicking ok. You can also double-click a template icon. Access opens the file new database dialog box and suggests a name for your new database file. You can modify the name and then click create to launch the wizard.

The wizard takes a few moments to initialize and to create a blank file for your new database application. The wizard first displays a page with a few more details about the capabilities of the application you are about to build. If this isn't what you want, click Cancel to close the wizard and delete the database file. You can click Finish to have the wizard quickly build the application with all the default options. Click Next to proceed to a window that provides options for customizing the tables in your application, as shown in the following illustration.

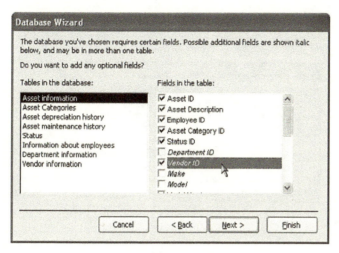

Fig 5.6

In this window, you can see the names of the tables the wizard plans to build. As you select each table name in the list on the left, the wizard shows you the fields it will include in that table in the list on the right. For many of the tables, you can have the wizard include or exclude certain optional fields (which appear in italic). In the Asset Tracking application, for example, you might be interested in keeping track of the vendor for each asset. When you click the optional Vendor ID field in the Asset information table, you'll be able to specify from which vendor you acquired the asset. Click Next when you finish selecting optional fields for your application.

In the next window, shown in the following illustration, you select one of several styles for the forms in your database. Forms are objects in your database that are used to display and edit data on your screen. As you click each style name, the Database Wizard shows you a sample of that style on the left. The Standard style has a very businesslike gray-on-gray look.

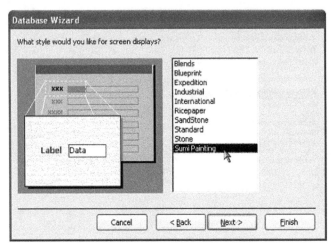

Fig 5.7

After you select a form style, click Next to proceed to the window to select a report style. You might want to select Bold, Casual, or Compact for personal applications. Corporate, Formal, and Soft Gray are good choices for business applications. Again, you can see a sample of the style on the left as you click on each available style on the right. Select an appropriate report style, and then click Next.

In the next page of the Database Wizard, you specify the title that will appear in the Access title bar when you run the application. You can also include a picture file such as a company logo in your reports. This picture file can be a bitmap (.bmp), a Windows metafile (.wmf), or an icon file (.ico). Click Next after you supply a title for your application.

In the final window, you can choose to start the application immediately after the wizard finishes building it. You can also choose to open a special set of Help topics to guide you through using a database application. Select the Yes, Start the database option and click Finish to create and then start your application.

Fig 5.8

Once you use one of the built-in templates, Access lists that template under Recently used templates in the New File task pane in case you want to use that template again.

5.3.3 Creating an empty database

To begin creating a new empty database when you start Access, on the File menu, click New, and then, in the New File task pane, click Blank Database. This opens the File New Database dialog box, shown in the following illustration.

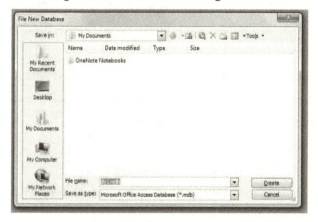

Fig 5.9

Select the drive and folder you want from the Save in drop-down list. In this example, select the My Documents folder on My Computer. Finally, go to the File name box and type the name of your new database. Access appends an .mdb extension to the file name for you. Click the Create button to create your database.

Access takes a few moments to create the system tables in which to store all the information about the tables, queries, forms, reports, data access pages, macros, and modules that you might create. After Access completes this process, it displays the Database window for your new database, as shown in the following diagram.

Fig 5.10

When you open a database, Access selects the button under Objects that you last chose in the Database window for that database. For example, if the last time you were in this database you worked on queries, Access highlights the Queries button on the left and shows you the last query that you selected in the pane on the right the next time you open the database. Each button under Objects displays the available objects of that type.

Because this is a new database and no tables or special startup settings exist yet, you see a Database window with no objects defined. The items you see under Tables are simply shortcuts to three ways to create a table.

5.4 Table creation

5.4.1 Creating your first simple table by entering data

Click the New button in the Database window to open the New Table dialog box, shown in the following illustration.

Fig 5.11

69

Select Datasheet View in the list, and then click OK to get started. What you see next is an empty datasheet, which looks quite similar to a spreadsheet. You can enter just about any type of data you want — text, dates, numbers, currency. But unlike in a spreadsheet, in a datasheet you can't enter any calculated expressions. However, you can easily display a calculated result using data from one or more tables by entering an expression in a query.

When you start to type in a field within a row, Access displays a pencil icon on the row selector at the far left to indicate that you're adding or changing data in that row. Use the TAB key to move from column to column. When you move to another row, Access saves what you typed. If you make a mistake in a particular row or column, you can click the data you want to change and type over it or delete it.

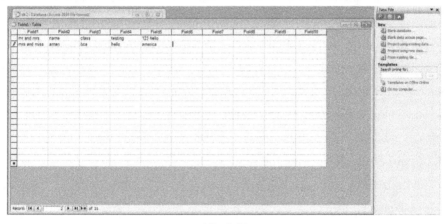

Fig 5.12

If you create a column of data that you don't want, click anywhere in the column and click Delete Column on the Edit menu. If you want to insert a blank column between two columns that already contain data, click anywhere in the column to the right of where you want to insert the new column and then click Column on the Insert menu. To move a column to a different location, click the field name at the top of the column to highlight the entire column, and then click again and drag the column to a new location. You can also click an unselected column and drag your mouse pointer

70

through several adjacent columns to highlight them all. You can then move the columns as a group.

After you enter several rows of data, you can save your table by clicking the Save button on the toolbar or by clicking Save on the File menu. Access displays a Save As dialog box, as shown in the following illustration.

Fig 5.13

Type an appropriate name for your table, and then click OK. Access displays a message box warning you that you have no primary key defined for this table and offering to build one for you. If you accept the offer, Access adds a field called ID and assigns it a special data type named AutoNumber that automatically generates a unique number for each new row you add. If one or more of the data columns you entered would make a good primary key, click No in the message box. In this case, click Yes to build a field called ID that will serve as the primary key.

5.4.2 Creating a table by using the Table Wzard

To build a table by using the Table Wizard, open the Database window, click the Tables button, and then click the New button. In the New Table dialog box, select Table Wizard from the list and click OK. You can also double-click the Create table by using wizard shortcut shown near the top of the Database window. You'll see the opening page of the Table Wizard, shown in the following illustration.

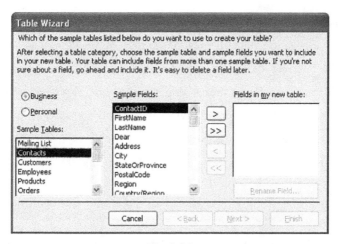

Fig 5.14

Toward the middle left of the window are two option buttons —Business and Personal. You can find an entry for a Contacts sample table in the Business category. When you select this table, the wizard displays all the fields from the Contacts sample table in the Sample Fields list.

To select a field, click its name in the Sample Fields list, and then click the single right arrow (>) button to move it to the Fields in my new table list. You define the sequence of fields in your table on the basis of the sequence in which you select them from the Sample Fields list. If you add a field that you decide you don't want, select it in the Fields in my new table list and click the single left arrow (<) button to remove it. If you want to start over, you can remove all fields by clicking the double left arrow (<<) button. If you pick fields in the wrong sequence, you must remove any field that is out of sequence: Click the field above where you want the field inserted, and then select that field again.

Many of the fields in the Contacts sample table are fields you'll need in the Contacts table for your Contact Tracking database. You can pick ContactID, FirstName, Last Name, Address, City, State Or Province, Postal Code, Country/Region, Work Phone, Work Extension, and Email Name directly from the Contacts sample table.

Now you need to rename some of the fields. Rename the first Address field to Work Address by clicking that field in the Fields in my new table list and then clicking the

72

Rename Field button. The Table Wizard opens a dialog box to allow you to type a new name. You need to rename the rest of the first set of address fields with a Work prefix, and then correct the names of the second set of fields to use as home address information by adding a Home prefix. While you're at it, also remove /Region from the Country/Region fields. The following illustration shows how to rename the second Birth date field to Spouse Birth Date. As you can see, it's easy to mix and match fields from various sample tables and then rename the fields to get exactly what you want.

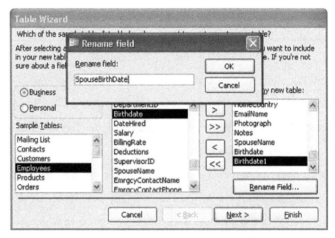

Fig 5.15

Click the Next button to see the window shown in the following illustration.

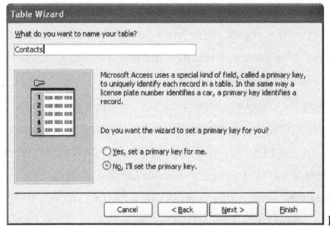

Fig 5.16

73

In this window, you can specify a name for your new table. You can also ask the wizard to set a primary key for you, or you can define your own primary key. In many cases, the wizard chooses the most logical field or fields to be the primary key, but you can override this by clicking the No, I'll set the primary key option. If the wizard can't find an appropriate field to be the primary key, it creates a new primary key field that uses a special data type called "AutoNumber." As you'll learn later in this article, the AutoNumber data type ensures that each new row in your table will have a unique value as its primary key.

Choose the option to pick your own primary key and then click Next. The Table Wizard appears, as shown below.

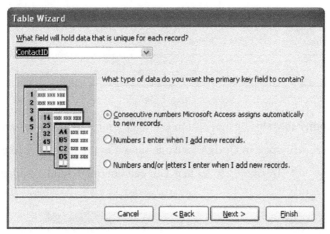

Fig 5.17

You can open the list at the top of the window to select any field that you defined.

Click the Next button to move to the next page of the wizard. If you have other tables already defined in your database, the Table Wizard shows you a list of those tables and tells you whether it thinks your new table is related to any of the existing tables. If the wizard finds a primary key in another table with the same name and data type as a field in your new table (or vice versa), it assumes that the tables are related. If you think the wizard has made a mistake, you can prevent it from creating a relationship (a link) between your new table and the existing table. Because this is the first and only table in this database, you won't see the

Relationships page in the Table Wizard. Instead, the wizard shows you a final page in which you can choose to modify the table design, open it as a datasheet, or call another wizard to build a form to edit your data, as shown in the following illustration.

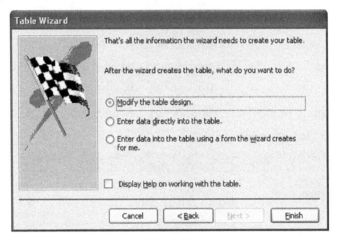

Fig 5.18

Select the Modify the table design option and click Finish to let the wizard build your table. The table will open in Design view, as shown in the following illustration. For now, close the table Design view so that you can continue building other tables that you need.

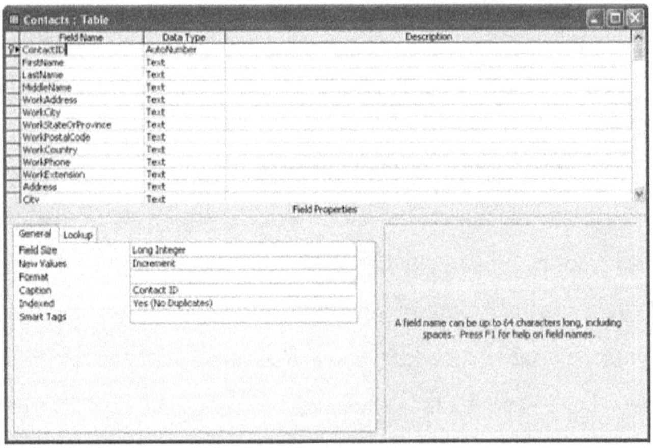

Fig 5.19

5.4.3 Creating a table in Design view

To design a new table in a database, open the Database window, as shown in the following illustration.

Fig 5.20

Click the Tables button under Objects, and then click the New button. Access displays the New Table dialog box. Select Design View and click OK. You can also double-click the Create table in Design view shortcut in the Database window. Access displays an empty table in Design view.

In Design view, the upper part of the table displays columns in which you can enter the field names, the data type for each field, and a description of each field. After you select a data type for a field, Access allows you to set field properties in the lower-left area of the table. In the lower-right area of the table is a box in which Access displays information about fields or properties. The contents of this box change as you move from one location to another within the table.

5.4.3.1 Access data types

Data type	Usage	Size
Text	Alphanumeric data	Up to 255 characters
Memo	Alphanumeric data, sentences and paragraphs	Up to about 1 gigabyte (but controls to display a memo

		are limited to the first 65,535 characters)
Number	Numeric data	1, 2, 4, 8, or 16 bytes
Date/Time	Dates and times	8 bytes
Currency	Monetary data, stored with 4 decimal places of precision	8 bytes
AutoNumber	Unique value generated by Access for each new record	4 bytes (16 bytes for Replication ID)
Yes/No	Boolean (true/false) data; Access stores the numeric value zero (0) for false, and minus one (-1) for true.	1 bit
OLE Object	Pictures, graphs, or other ActiveX objects from another Windows-based application	Up to about 2 gigabytes
Hyperlink	A link address to a document or file on the World Wide Web, on an intranet, on a local area network (LAN), or on your local computer	Up to about 1 gigabyte

Fig 5.21

Access also gives you a tenth option, Lookup Wizard, to help you define the characteristics of foreign key fields that link to other tables.

For each field in your table, select the data type that is best suited to how you will use that field's data. For character data, you should normally select the Text data type. You can control the maximum length of a Text field by using a field property, as explained later. Use the Memo data type only for long strings of text that might exceed 255 characters or that might contain formatting characters such as tabs or line endings (carriage returns).

When you select the Number data type, you should think carefully about what you enter as the Field Size property because this property choice will affect precision as well as length. (For example, integer numbers do not have decimals.) The Date/Time data type is useful for calendar or clock data and has the added benefit of allowing calculations in seconds, minutes, hours, days, months, or years. For example, you can find out the difference in days between two Date/Time values.

You should generally use the Currency data type for storing money values. Currency has the precision of integers, but with exactly four decimal places. When you need to store a precise fractional number that's not money, use the Number data type and choose Decimal for the Field Size property.

The AutoNumber data type is specifically designed for automatic generation of primary key values. Depending on the settings for the Field Size and New Values properties you choose for an AutoNumber field, you can have Access create a sequential or random long integer. You can include only one field using the AutoNumber data type in any table. If you define more than one AutoNumber field, Access displays an error message when you try to save the table.

Use the Yes/No data type to hold Boolean (true or false) values. This data type is particularly useful for flagging accounts paid or not paid or orders filled or not filled.

The OLE Object data type allows you to store complex data, such as pictures, graphs, or sounds, which can be edited or displayed through a dynamic link to another Windows-based application. For example, Access can store and allow you to edit a Microsoft Word document, a Microsoft Excel spreadsheet, a Microsoft PowerPoint presentation slide, a sound file (.wav), a video file (.avi), or pictures created using the Microsoft Paint or Draw application.

The Hyperlink data type lets you store a simple or complex "link" to an external file or document. (Internally, Hyperlink is a memo data type with a special flag set to indicate that it is a link.) This link can contain a Uniform Resource Locator (URL) that points to a location on the World Wide Web or on a local intranet. It can also contain the Universal Naming Convention (UNC) name of a file on a server on your local area network (LAN) or on your local computer drives. The link can point to a file that is in Hypertext Markup Language (HTML) or in a format that is supported by an ActiveX application on your computer.

5.4.3.2 Setting field properties

You can customize the way Access stores and handles each field by setting specific properties. These properties vary according to the data type you choose. The following table lists all the possible properties that can appear on a field's General tab in a table's Design view, and the data types that are associated with each property.

Field properties on the General tab

DATA TYPE	OPTIONS, DESCRIPTION
Field Size Property	
Text	Text can be from 0 through 255 characters long, with a default length of 50 characters.
Number	Byte A single-byte integer containing values from 0 through 255.
	Integer A 2-byte integer containing values from -32,768 through +32,767.
	Long Integer A 4-byte integer containing values from -2,147,483,648 through +2,147,483,647.
	Single A 4-byte floating-point number containing values from -3.4E+38 through +3.4E+38 and up to seven significant digits.
	Double An 8-byte floating-point number containing values from -1.797E+308 through 1.797E+308 and up to 15 significant digits.
	Replication ID A 16-byte globally unique identifier (GUID).
	Decimal A 12-byte integer with a defined decimal precision that can contain values from -1E+28 through 1E+28. The default precision (number of decimal places) is 0 and the

default scale is 18.

AutoNumber	Long Integer A 4-byte integer containing values from -2,147,483,648 through +2,147,483,647 when New Values is Random or from 1 to +2,147,483,647 when New Values is Increment.
	Replication ID A 16-byte globally unique identifier (GUID).

New Values Property

AutoNumber only	Increment Values start at 1 and increment by 1 for each new row.
	Random Access assigns a random long integer value to each new row.

Format Property

Text, Memo	You can specify a custom format that controls how Access displays the data. For details about custom formats, see the article Format Property - Text and Memo Data Types, at the Microsoft Developer Network (MSDN) Library.
Number (except Replication ID), Currency, AutoNumber	General Number (default) No commas or currency symbols; the number of decimal places shown depends on the precision of the data.
	Currency Currency symbol (from the regional settings in Windows Control Panel) and two decimal places.
	Euro Euro currency symbol (regardless of Control Panel settings) and two decimal places.
	Fixed At least one digit and two decimal places.

Standard Two decimal places and separator commas.

Percent Percentage — moves displayed decimal point two places to the right and appends a percentage (%) symbol.

Scientific Scientific notation (for example, 1.05E+06 represents 1.05×106).

You can specify a custom format that controls how Access displays the data. For details about custom formats, see the article Format Property - Number and Currency Data Types, at the MSDN Library.

Date/Time	General Date (default) Combines Short Date and Long Time format (for example, 4/15/2003 5:30:10 PM).

Long Date Uses Long Date Style from the regional settings in Windows Control Panel (for example, Tuesday, April 15, 2003).

Medium Date 15-Apr-2003.

Short Date Uses Short Date Style from the regional settings in Windows Control Panel (for example, 4/15/ 2003).

Long Time Uses Time Style from the regional settings in Windows Control Panel (for example, 5:30:10 PM).

Medium Time 5:30 PM.

Short Time 17:30.

You can specify a custom format that controls how Access displays the data. For details about custom formats, see the article Format Property - Date/Time Data Type, at the MSDN Library.

Yes/No	Yes/No (default)

True/False

On/Off

You can specify a custom format that controls how Access displays the data. For details about custom formats, see the article Format Property - Yes/No Data Type, at the MSDN Library.

Precision Property

Number, Decimal	You can specify the maximum number of digits allowed. The default value is 18, and you can specify an integer value between 1 and 28.

Scale Property

Number, Decimal	You can specify the number of decimal digits stored. This value must be less than or equal to the value of the Precision property.

Decimal Places Property

Number (except Replication ID), Currency	You can specify the number of decimal places that Access displays. The default specification is Auto, which causes Access to display two decimal places for the Currency, Fixed, Standard, and Percent formats and the number of decimal places necessary to show the current precision of the numeric value for General Number format. You can also request a fixed display of decimal places ranging from 0 through 15.

Input Mask Property

Text, Number (except	You can specify an editing mask that the user sees while

Replication	ID),	entering data in the field. For example, you can have
Date/Time, Currency		Access provide the delimiters in a date field such as __/ __/__, or you can have Access format a U.S. phone number as (###) 000-0000. See the section Defining input masks for details.

Caption Property

All	You can enter a more fully descriptive field name that Access displays in form labels and in report headings. Tip If you create field names with no embedded spaces, you can use the Caption property to specify a name that includes spaces for Access to use in labels and headers associated with this field in queries, forms, and reports.

Default   Value Property

Text, Memo, Date/ Time, Hyperlink, Yes/No	You can specify a default value for the field that Access automatically uses for a new row if no other value is supplied. If you don't specify a default value, the field will be Null if the user fails to supply a value. See also the Required property.
Number, Currency	Access sets the property to 0. You can change the setting to a valid numeric value. You can also remove the setting, in which case the field will be Null if the user fails to supply a value. See also the Required property.

Validation   Rule Property

All (except OLE Object, Replication	You can supply an expression that must be true whenever you enter or change data in this field. For

ID, and AutoNumber)	example, <100 specifies that a number must be less than 100. You can also check for one of a series of values. For example, you can have Access check for a list of valid cities by specifying "Chicago" Or "New York" Or "San Francisco". In addition, you can specify a complex expression that includes any of the built-in functions in Access
Validation Text Property	
All (except OLE Object, Replication ID, and AutoNumber)	You can specify a custom message that Access displays whenever the data entered does not pass your validation rule.
Required Property	
All (except AutoNumber)	If you don't want to allow a Null value for the field, set this property to Yes.
Allow Zero Length Property	
Text, Memo	You can set the field equal to a zero-length string ("") if you set this property to Yes.
Indexed Property	
All except OLE Object	You can ask that an index be built to speed access to data values. You can also require that the values in the indexed field always be unique for the entire table.
Unicode Compression Property	

Text, Memo, Hyperlink	As of version 2000, Access stores character fields in an .mdb file using a double-byte (Unicode) character set to support extended character sets in languages that require them. The Latin character set required by most Western European languages (such as English, Spanish, French, or German) requires only one byte per character. When you set Unicode Compression to Yesfor character fields, Access stores compressible characters in one byte instead of two, thus saving space in your database file. However, Access will not compress Memo or Hyperlink fields that will not compress to fewer than 4,096 bytes.
IME Mode Property, IME Sentence Mode Property	
Text, Memo, Hyperlink	On machines with an Asian version of Windows and appropriate Input Method Editor (IME) installed, these properties control conversion of characters in Kanji, Hiragana, Katakana, and Hangul character sets.
Smart Tags Property	
All data types except Yes/No, OLE Object, and Replication ID	Indicates the registered smart tag name and action that you want associated with this field. When the user views this field in a table datasheet, a query datasheet, or a form, Access displays a smart tag available indicator next to the field. The user can click on the indicator and select the smart tag action to perform.

Fig 5.22

5.5 Queries in MS ACCESS

5.5.1) Defining SQL Queries in Access and Built-in Arithmetic Functions

SQL is a standardized way to query or ask a question about what's in a data base. The same kind of syntax is used in many different database systems like Access, Oracle, MySQL, etc. It is essential to understand SQL if you want to be able to embed queries in a programming language. We will do this later when we retrieve data from a database by embedding SQL queries in a JSP program. The combination of SQL with a programming language provides a powerful tool which allows one to flexibly process the information in a database. The following examples are more 'hardwired' than queries in a JSP. Here, the attribute values are explicitly specified, while in a program they would usually be variables.

The SQL queries utilize the following core syntax:

SELECT   the data or attributes wanted for the answer

FROM   database tables needed to handle the query

WHERE   Boolean restrictions are specified which depend on the question, as well as interlinking-conditions - for the tables needed to answer the query based on their shared attributes

To define an SQL query in Access, click Queries under Objects in the dialog window, then click 'Create query in Design view'. For simplicity, close the 'show table' dialog window' that opens, but leave the 'Select Query' window open. Click the SQL tab on the uppermost, top left toolbar for Access (the outermost window you are working with) and select SQL View on the pop-down menu, which will clear the 'Select Query' window so it just contains 'Select;'. Then enter the desired SQL query in this text area. For example, you can begin with a query that retrieves all (the information on) the Books where the author is 'Aman' as follows:

Select * From Books as bWhere b.author = 'Aman'

In this example, the notation '*' means that all the attribute values of the rows that satisfy the Where condition are to be returned or displayed. In this example, the only table involved is Books, which we have given the shorthand name b (just like an algebraic variable.)   In order to execute the query, click the red exclamation point (!

86

) that appears after you have entered the query on the topmost Access toolbar, to execute query. (This requires the Query dialog window to have had at least a <CR> entered in order for the ! to be accessible.)

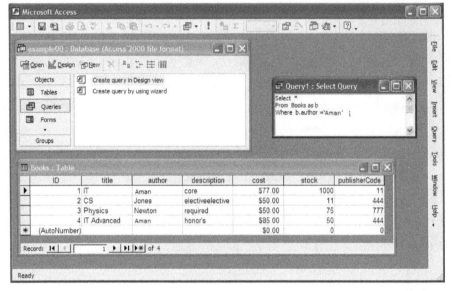

Fig 5.23

The query returns the requested results in a table as shown below. To see the original query again, right click the data table on the title bar and select SQL View. If you close the Query-1 window, you will be asked at that point if you want to save it (for future reference). It is important to verify the correctness of the query results – certainly at least when the query is first being tested. It is easy to incorrectly define a query that looks or appears to right because it gives the right answers. But the query may actually be wrongly formulated. For example, it may also give extraneous answers in addition to the correct ones, or it may omits some of the correct answers. Remember that the answer is only correct if it supplies the whole truth and nothing but the truth. Supplying some of the correct answers is not enough; adding in some incorrect answers as well won't do either.

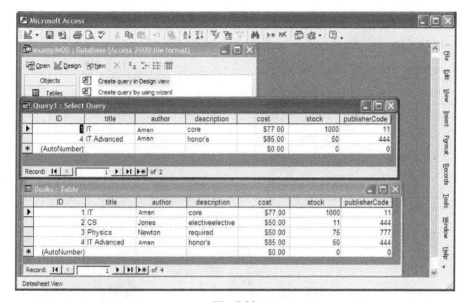

Fig 5.23

To selectively retrieve attributes, we list the desired attributes in the Select clause:

Select title, cost From Books as b Where b.author = 'Aman'

In this case a two-column table with title & cost attributes is returned, with rows that satisfy the Where clause condition.   Caveat: Because the Access data font is small, it's easy to inadvertently introduce, for example, a leading blank before the data (such as in typing ' Aman' by mistake). In such a case, the string ' Aman' would not match the string 'Aman' (since the actual data presumably does not have the leading blank), so an empty table would be returned. It is also easy to overlook having introduced a space before the dot in expressions like b.author (such as b .author). This will trigger a popup prompt for a parameter value which is actually irrelevant.   Misspelling attribute names also triggers the same indirect manifestation of an error.

To retrieve all authors other than 'Aman' use the Not operator:

Select title, cost From Books as b Where Not (b.author = 'Aman')

which means the same as: author is not 'Aman'.

The Where clause can also be omitted as in the following query:

Select   title, author From Books as b

In which case all the title/author entries in the table are retrieved without qualification.

The syntax for using mathematical formulas in is easy and natural. For example, if you want to retrieve the dollar value of the inventory per book where 'Aman' is the author, the cost per book and the number of books should be multiplied as in:

Select title, b.cost * b.stock From Books as b Where b.author = 'Aman'

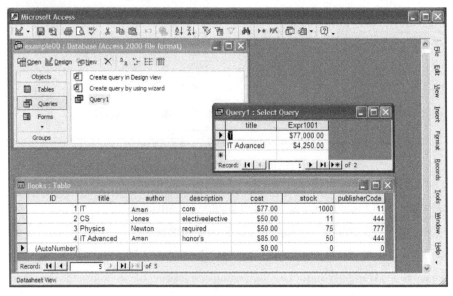

Fig 5.24

To determine the total value of the inventory over all such books, we use the built-in function Sum applied to the formula:

Select Sum (b.cost * b.stock) From Books as b Where b.author = 'Aman'

which returns the results in the snapshot shown below. Additional examples of arithmetic calculations are given in the baseball database below.

The MS Access arithmetic capability can be embedded in JSP programs to facilitate accounting style calculations by relying on built-in services provided by Access. This is quite important since it means that you can let SQL queries embedded in your JSP program perform potentially complex calculations without having to write the algorithms yourself in Java. The SQL lets you obtain these effects using simple imperative descriptions of what you want to calculate with almost no effort on your part except the formulation of the SQL statement.

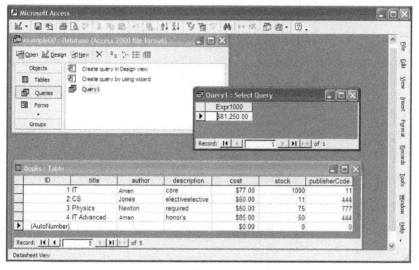

Fig 5.25

Exercise

Q1. How you create table in MS Access?

Q2. Explain different type of data types.

Q3. What is primary key.

Q4.What is query ?

Q5.Implement query on table.

CHAPTER 6 Advance Features in DBMS

6.1 Applying Integrity Constraints

Constraints are a very important feature in a relational model. In fact, the relational model supports well defined theory of constraints on attributes or tables. Constraints are useful because they allow a designer to specify the semantics of data in the database and constraints are the rules to enforce DBMSs to check that data satisfies the semantics.

6.1.1 Domain Integrity

Domain restricts the values of attributes in the relation and it is a constraint of the relational model. However, there are real –world semantics on data that cannot specified if used only with domain constraints. We need more specific ways to state what data values are/are not allowed and what format is suitable for an attributes. For example, the employee ID must be unique, the employee birthday is in the range [Jan 1, 1950, Jan 1, 2000]. Such information is provided in logical statements called integrity constraints.

There are several kinds of integrity constraints:

6.1.2 Entity Integrity – Every table requires a primary key. The primary key, nor any part of the primary key, can contain NULL values. This is because NULL values for the primary key means we cannot identify some rows. For example, in the EMPLOYEE table, Phone cannot be a key since some people may not have a phone.

6.1.3 Referential integrity – a foreign key must have a matching primary key or it must be null. This constraint is specified between two tables (parent and child); it maintains the correspondence between rows in these tables. It means the reference from a row in one table to other table must be valid. Examples of Referential integrity constraint:

Referential integrity Examples

In the Customer/Order database:

- Customer(**custid**, custname)
- Order(**orderID**, custid, OrderDate)

To ensure that there are no orphan records, we need to enforce referential integrity.

An orphan record is one whose foreign key value is not found in the corresponding entity – the entity where the PK is located. Recall that a typical join is between a PK and FK.

The referential integrity constraint states that the CustID in the Order table must match a valid CustiD in the Customer table. Most relational databases have declarative referential integrity. In other words, when the tables are created the referential integrity constraints are set up.

In the Course/Class database:

- Course(**CrsCode**, DeptCode, Description)
- Class(**CrsCode, Section**, ClassTime)

The referential integrity constraint states that CrsCode in the Class table must match a valid CrsCode in the Course table. In this situation, it's not enough that the CrsCode and Section in the Class table make up the PK, we must also enforce referential integrity.

When setting up referential integrity it is important that the PK and FK have the same data types and come from the same domain. Otherwise the RDBMS will not allow the join.

Referential Integrity in MS Access

In MS Access referential integrity is set up by joining the PK in the Customer table to the CustID in the Order table.

CREATE TABLE Customer

(CustID INTEGER PRIMARY KEY,

CustName CHAR(35)

)

CREATE TABLE Orders

(OrderID INTEGER PRIMARY KEY,

CustID INTEGER REFERENCES Customer(CustID),

OrderDate DATETIME

)

The referential integrity is set when creating the table (Orders) with the FK.

Foreign Key Rules

Additional foreign key rules may be added, such as what to do with the child rows (Orders table) when the record with the PK – the parent (Customer) is deleted or changed (updated). The relationship window in Access shows two additional options for foreign keys rules. Cascade Update and Cascade Delete. If they are not selected, the system would prevent the deletion or update of PK values in the parent table (Customer) if a child record exists. The child record is any record with a matching PK.

DELETE

- RESTRICT

- CASCADE

- SET TO NULL

UPDATE

- RESTRICT

- CASCADE

In some databases, an additional option exists when selecting the Delete option. That is 'Set to Null'. In these situations, the PK row is deleted, but the FK in the child table is set to Null. Though this creates an orphan row, it is acceptable.

Enterprise Constraints – sometimes referred to as Semantic constraints. They are additional rules specified by users or database administrators. i.e. A class can have a maximum of 30 students. A teacher can teach a maximum of 4 classes a semester. An employee cannot take a part in more than 5 projects. Salary of an employee cannot exceed the salary of the employee's manager.

Business Rules

Another term we've used is semantics. Business rules are obtained from users when gathering requirements. The requirements gathering process is very important and should be verified by the user before the database design is built. If the business rules are incorrect, the design will be incorrect and ultimately the application built will not function as expected by the users.

Some examples of business rules are:

- A teacher can teach many students
- A class can have a maximum of 35 students
- A course can be taught many times, but by only one instructor
- Not all teachers teach classes, etc.

Cardinality

Expresses minimum and maximum number of entity occurrences associated with one occurrence of related entity. Business rules are used to determine cardinality.

There are two sides to each of the relationships when it comes to participation. Each side can have two options for participation. It is either 0 (zero), 1 (one), or many. The outer most symbol represents the connectivity.

The inner most symbols represent the cardinality which indicates the minimum number of instances in the corresponding entity. i.e. on the right hand side it is read as: minimum 1 maximum many. On the left hand side it's read as minimum 1 and maximum 1.

Optional

One entity occurrence does not require a corresponding entity occurrence in a relationship

This can also be read as:

Right hand side: A customer can be in a minimum of 0 orders or a maximum of many orders.

Left hand side: The order entity must contain a minimum of one related entity in the customer table and a maximum of 1 related entity.

Mandatory

One entity occurrence requires a corresponding entity occurrence in a relationship

However, it cannot have a connectivity of 0 only 1 (as shown). The connectivity symbols show maximums. So if you think about it logically, if the connectivity symbol on the left hand side shows 0, then there would be no connection between the tables. The way to read the left hand side is: The CustID in the Order table must be found in the Customer table a minimum of 0 and a maximum of 1 time. The 0 means that the CustID in the Order table may be null. The left most 1 (right before the 0 representing connectivity) says that if there is a CustID in the Order table it can only be in the Customer table once. When you see the 0 symbol for cardinality you can assume two things. The FK in the Order table allows nulls, and the FK is not part of the PK since PKs must not contain null values.

Introduction to forms

6.2 Creating a form

To create a form we need to position ourselves in the database window with the Form object selected, if we then click on the New button a window opens with the various ways we have to create a form as you can see in the below fig 6.1:

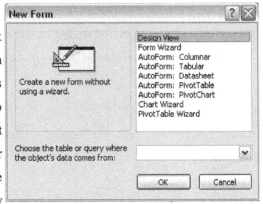

1. Design view opens a blank form in design view, and we then need to incorporate the various object that we would like to appear in it. This method is not used much as it is easier and faster to create an autoform, or to use the wizard and afterward modify the design of the created form to adjust it to our needs. We will see ahead in this sunit how to modify the form design.

2. Form wizard uses an a wizard that guides us step by step in the creation of the form.

3. Auto form consists of automatically creating a new form that contains all the data from the source table.

According to the type of form that we select (columnar, tabular,...) the form will present the data in a distinct way, when we click on one of the options, a sample will appear on the left side with the way in which the data will be presented with this option. E.g Auto form: columnar presents one record on a screen, meanwhile Auto form: tabular presents all the records on one screen and every record in a row.

95

In order to use this function we first need to fill out the Choose the table or query where the object's data comes from: with the name of the source. This will be the only data to introduce, and once introduced we select the kind of autoform and click on OK button, and Access does the rest.

4. Chart Wizard uses a wizard that guides us step by step in the creation of a graphic.

5. Pivot table wizard uses a wizard that guides us step by step in the creation of dynamic table.

6.3 The Form's wizard

To start the wizard we can do it as describe in the last point, or a faster way would be from the Database window with the Forms object selected, by double clicking on the Create form using wizard option.

You can create a form on your own or you can have Microsoft Access create your form for you using a Form Wizard. A Form Wizard speeds up the process of creating a form because it does all the basic work for you. When you use a Form Wizard, Microsoft Access prompts you for information and creates a form based on your answers. Even if you've created many forms, you may want to use a Form Wizard to quickly lay out all the controls on your form. Then you can switch to Design view to customize your form.

Forms are designed to ease the data entry process. For example, you can create a data entry form that looks exactly like a paper form. People generally prefer to enter data into a well-designed form, rather than a table.

To start the wizard we can do it as describe in the last point, or a faster way would be from the Database window with the Forms object selected, by double clicking on the Create form using wizard option.

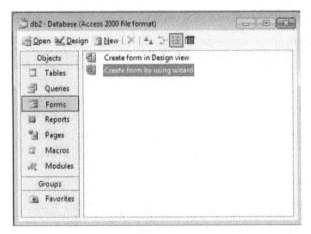

Fig 6.1

The first window of the wizard appears

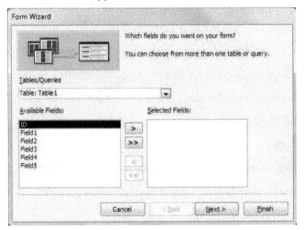

Fig 6.2

In this window we are asked to introduce the fields to include in the form.

Firstly we select from the Table/Queries box the table or query that we are going to get the data from, this will be the form source. If we want to extract data from various tables it would be better to first create a query to obtain this data and then select this query as the form source.

Next we will select the fields to include in the form by clicking on the field and then the

(>) button or simply double click on the field.

If we selected the wrong field click on the (<) button and the field will be removed from ther selected fields list.

We can select all the fields at the same time by clicking on the (>>) button or deselect all the fields at once using the button (<<).

Next we click on the Next button and the window seen in the following example will appear.

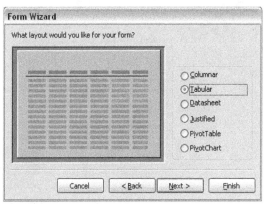

Fig 6.3

In this screen we select the data distribution within the form. By selecting a format it will appear on the left side the way it will be seen in the form.

Once we have selected the distribution of our choice click Next and the following window will appear:

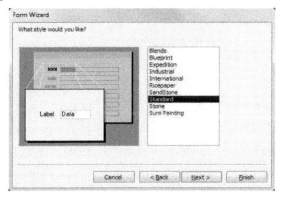

Fig 6.4

In this screen we select the forms style, we can select between the various defined styles that Access has. By selecting a style it will appear on the left side as it will in the form.

Once we have selected a style of our choice we click on the Next button and the last screen of the forms wizard will appear.

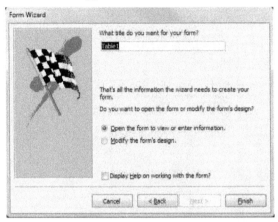

Fig 6.5

In this window we are asked for the title of the form, this title will also be the name assigned to the form.

Before clicking on the Finish button we can choose between

Fig 6.6

To edit the data of a table using a form, we need to open the form by positioning ourselves in the Database window with the Forms object selected and click on the open button, or simply double click on the name of the form in the Database window. The source data of the form will appear with the appearance defined in the form (Form view). We can then search for data using the navigation buttons , replace values, and modify it as if we were in the Datasheet view of a table, the only thing that changes is the appearance of the screen.

6.4 Sorting and Filtering

6.4.1 Filter by Selection

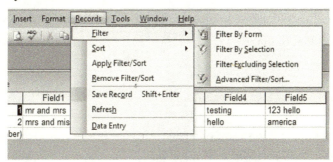

Fig 6.7

1.   Start Microsoft Access, and then open the database that you are working with.

2.   In a field on a form, a subform, a datasheet, or a subdatasheet, select one instance of the value that you want to filter by (for example, a name or a number).

3.   On the Records menu, point to Filter, and then click Filter by Selection.

4.   Repeat steps 2 and 3 until you have the set of records that you are looking for.NOTE: You can also filter for records that do not have a certain value. After you select a value, right-click, and then click Filter Excluding Selection.

6.4.2 Filter by Form

1.   Open a form in Form view, or a table, a query, or a form in Datasheet view. To filter records in a subdatasheet, display the subdatasheet by clicking its expand indicator.

2.   On the Records menu, point to Filter, and then click Filter By Form to switch to the Filter By Form window.

3.   You can specify criteria for the form, the subform, the main datasheet, or any subdatasheet that is displayed. Each subform or subdatasheet has its own Look For and Or tabs.

4.   Click the field in which you want to specify the criteria.

5.   Enter your criteria by selecting the value that you are searching for from the list in the field (if the list includes field values), or by typing the value into the field. To find records in which a particular field is empty or not empty, type Is Null or Is Not Null into the field.

6.   To specify additional values that records can have in the filter, click the Or tab for the form, the subform, the datasheet, or the sub datasheet that you are filtering, and then enter more criteria.

7.   On the Filter menu, click Apply Filter to view the filter results.

6.4.3 Filter for Input

1.   Open a form in Form view, or a table, a query, or a form in Datasheet view. To filter records in a subdatasheet, display the subdatasheet by clicking its expand indicator.

2.   Right-click in the field in the form, the subform, the datasheet, or the subdatasheet that you are filtering, and then type the value that you are looking for in the Filter For box on the shortcut menu.

3.   Press ENTER to apply the filter, and then close the shortcut menu.

6.4.4 Advanced Filter/Sort

1.   Open a form in Form view, or a table, a query, or a form in Datasheet view.

2.   Click in the form, the subform, the datasheet, or the subdatasheet that you want to filter.

3.   On the Records menu, point to Filter, and then click Advanced Filter/Sort.

4.   Add the fields that you need to specify the values or the other criteria that the filter will use to find records to the design grid.

5.   To specify a sort order, click in the Sort cell for a field, click the arrow, and then select a sort order. Microsoft Access first sorts the leftmost field in the design grid, and then it sorts the next field to the right, and so on.

6.   In the Criteria cell for the fields that you have included, enter the value that you are looking for or enter an expression.

7.   On the Filter menu, click Apply Filter to view the filter's results.

6.5 Controls

Microsoft Access includes the following types of controls, which are all accessible through the toolbox in Design view of a form, report, or data access page: text box, label, option group, option button, check box, list box, command button, tab control, image control, line, rectangle, and ActiveX custom controls. You can also add a Microsoft Office PivotTable list, an Office Chart, or an Office Spreadsheet to a form, report, or data access page.

Forms and reports have these additional controls: toggle button, combo box, bound object frame, unbound object frame, and page break. You can also add a subform or subreport to a form or report. Data access pages also include the drop-down list box, hyperlinks, scrolling text, and the PivotTable list, spreadsheet, and chart components.

Controls are objects on a form, report, or data access page that display data, perform actions, or are used for decoration. For example, you can use a text box on a form, report, or data access page to display data, a command button on a form to open another form or report, or a line or rectangle to separate and group controls to make them more readable.

All the information on a form or report is contained in controls. On data access pages, information is contained in controls in the same way as it is on forms and reports. However, information can also be typed directly on the data access page.

6.5.1 Controls that you can use to display, enter, filter, or organize data in Access

1.   Text boxes

You use text boxes on a form, report, or data access page to display data from a record source. This type of text box is called a bound text box because it's bound to data in a field. Text boxes can also be unbound. For example, you can create an unbound text box to display the results of a calculation or to accept input from a user. Data in an unbound text box isn't stored anywhere.

2.   Labels

You use labels on a form, report, or data access page to display descriptive text such as titles, captions, or brief instructions. Labels don't display values from fields or expressions; they're always unbound and they don't change as you move from record to record.

A label can be attached to another control. When you create a text box, for example, it has an attached label that displays a caption for that text box. This label appears as a column heading in the Datasheet view of a form. When you create a label by using the Label tool , the label stands on its own — it isn't attached to any other control. You use stand-alone labels for information such as the title of a form, report, or data access page, or for other descriptive text. Stand-alone labels don't appear in Datasheet view.

3.　　List boxes, combo boxes and drop-down list boxes

List boxes The list in a list box consists of rows of data. In a form, a list box can have one or more columns, which can appear with or without headings. If a multiple-column list box is bound, Access stores the values from one of the columns. In a data access page, a list box has one column without a heading.

Combo boxes　　A combo box is like a text box and a list box combined, so it requires less room. You can type new values in it, as well as select values from a list. The list in a combo box consists of rows of data. Rows can have one or more columns, which can appear with or without headings.

When you enter text or select a value in a bound combo box, the entered or selected value is inserted into the field that the combo box is bound to. If a multiple-column combo box is bound, Access stores only the value from the bound column. You can use an unbound combo box to store a value that you can use with another control. For example, you could use an unbound combo box to limit the values in another combo box or in a custom dialog box. You could also use an unbound combo box to find a record based on the value you select in the combo box.

Drop-down list boxes On a data access page, you can use a drop-down list box instead of a list box. A drop-down list box on a data access page looks like a combo box on a form. As in a combo box, a drop-down list box shows only one record until you click to expand the contents; however, you can't type new values in a drop-down list box. The list in a drop-down list box consists of rows of data. Rows can have only one column that appears without headings.

When you select a value in a drop-down list box that is bound to a field, the selected value is inserted into that field. You can also use an unbound drop-down list box to store a value that you can use with another control. For example, you could use an unbound drop-down list box to limit the values in another drop-down list box. You could also use an unbound drop-down list box to find a record based on the value you select in the drop-down list box.

4.   Command buttons

Command buttons provide you with a way of performing action(s) by simply clicking them. When you choose the button, it not only carries out the appropriate action, it also looks as if it's being pushed in and released.

You use a command button on a form or data access page to start an action or a set of actions. For example, you can create a command button that opens another form. To make a command button do something on a form, you write a macro or event procedure and attach it to the button's OnClick property. On a data access page, you can attach code written in either Microsoft JScript or Microsoft Visual Basic Scripting Edition (VBScript) to a command button by using the Microsoft Script Editor.

You can display text or a picture on a command button in a form; you can display only text on a command button in a data access page.

You can create a command button on your own, or you can have Microsoft Access create your command button for you by using a wizard. A wizard speeds up the process of creating a command button because it does all the basic work for you. When you use a wizard, Access prompts you for information and then creates the command button based on your answers. By using the wizard, you can create more than 30 different types of command buttons. You can create command buttons to:

•   Dial a phone number.

•   Run a query or macro.

•   Run or quit an application.

- Edit or apply a filter.
- Print or mail a report.
- Print the current record.
- Update form data.
- Find a specific record.

5. Check Boxes

You can use a check box on a form, report, or data access page as a stand-alone control to display a Yes/No value from an underlying table, query, or SQL statement. For example, the check box in the following illustration is bound to the Discontinued field in the Products table. The data type of the Discontinued field is Yes/No. If the box contains a check mark, the value is Yes; if it doesn't, the value is No.

When you select or clear a check box that's bound to a Yes/No field in a Microsoft Access database or a Bit column in an Access project, Access displays the value in the underlying table according to the field's Format property (Yes/No, True/False, or On/Off). In an Access project, the option button is bound to a column defined as a Bit data type. When the value in this column is 1, it is equivalent to Yes, On, or True conditions. When the value is 0, the column indicates No, Off, or False conditions.

6. Option Buttons

You can use an option button on a form, report, or data access page as a stand-alone control to display a Yes/No value from an underlying record source. For example, the option button in the following illustration is bound to the Discontinued field in the Products table of a database. The data type of the Discontinued field is Yes/No. If the option button is selected, the value is Yes; if not, the value is No.

When you select or clear an option button that's bound to a Yes/No field in a Microsoft Access database, the value in the underlying table displays according to the field's Format property (Yes/No, True/False, or On/Off). In a Microsoft Access project, the option button is bound to a column defined as a Bit data type. When the value in this column is 1, it is equivalent to Yes, On, or True conditions. When the value is 0, the column indicates No, Off, or False conditions. You can also use option buttons in an option group to display values to choose from.

Exercise

Q1. What is Sorting and Filtering?

Q2. What is Referential integrity constraints?

Q3. Write down the steps to create Form in Ms.Access?

Q4. What is label and text box?

Q5. What is checkbox and radio button?

Chapter 7 Reports

7.1 Creating Reports

Reports are generally used to present the data of a table or query in order to print them. The basic difference with reports is that the data can only be visualized or printed (it can not be edited) and the information can be grouped and totals extracted by group more easily.

To start the wizard we can use the method explained in the previous point or a faster and easier method would be from the Database window with the Reports object selected to double click on the Create report by using wizard option

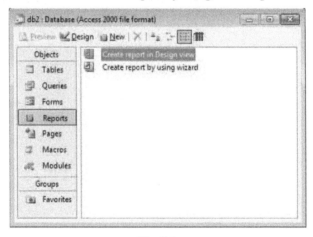

Fig 7.1

Formatted template used to print reports of database or query results. Allows user to specify fields, grouping levels, arrangement of printed data.

The wizard's first window will appear:

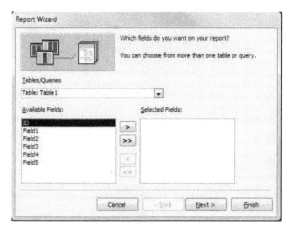

Fig 7.2

Firstly we select the table or query from the Tables/Queries box where it should extract the data from, this will be the report source. If we want to extract data from various fields it would be best to create a query to obtain the data and then to use this query as the source of the report. Next we select the fields by clicking on the field and then on the (>)button, or simply double clicking on the field.

If we make a mistake we click on the (<)button and the field will be removed from the list of selected fields. We can select all the fields at the same time by clicking on the (>>)button, or deselect all at the same time by clicking on the (<<)button.

Click on the Next button

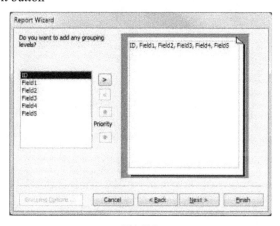

Fig 7.3

Click the Next Button

In the below screen we can choose to sort the fields into up to four sort fields. We select the field by which we choose to sort the records that will appear in the report and whether we want it in ascending or descending order, in order to select descending we click on the Ascending button and it will change to Descending.

We can select a different order in each of the sort fields

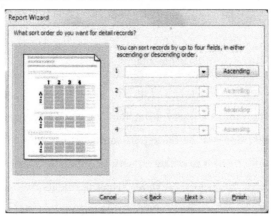

Fig 7.4

To continue with the wizard we click on the Next button and the following window will appear.

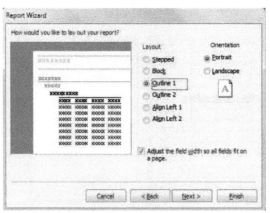

Fig 7.5

In this screen we select the type of style we would like our report to have, we can select from the various defined Access styles. By selecting a style the aspect that this report will take with this style will appear in the diagram to the left.Once we have selected a style we click on the Next button and the wizards last screen will appear.

Fig 7.6

In this screen we are asked the title of the report which will also be the name assigned to the report. After that click the finish button to see the report.

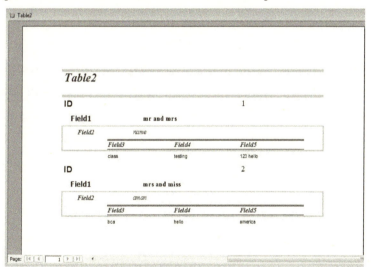

Fig 7.7

7.2 Macros

Macros are terrific for automating repetitive tasks but they also work really well when adding automation to your Access forms. For instance, with a macro, you can create a button on a form that opens another form or closes the open form which allows you to add a little bit of interactivity, or automation, for your users.

All macros are designed from the Macro window.

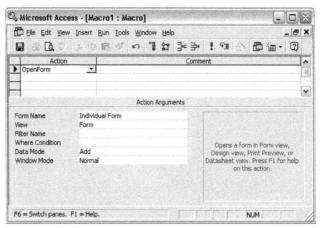

Fig 7.8

Use the dropdown menu to select your second action - choose "GoToRecord". In the bottom pane, choose the record you want to go to - choose "New". What we're doing here is ensuring that the form doesn't open up a previous record - it goes straight to the end and has a blank record ready for you to enter a new record

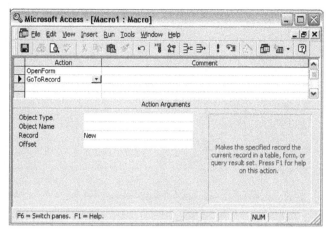

Fig 7.9

You're now ready to save your macro. To do this, click on the "Save" icon and enter a name for your macro. Make sure you name this macro "Autoexec". By naming it Autoexec, we are instructing Access to run this macro every time we open the database.

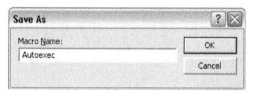

Fig 7.10

Testing your Macro

Close your database and then open it again. You will notice that when you open it, the Individual Form automatically opens and is ready for you to enter a new record. You can also run macros by opening the Macros tab and double clicking on the macro you want to run.

Exercise:

Q1. What is report?

Q2. Write down the steps to create report in Ms Access.

Q3. What is Macro?

Q4. Write down the steps to create and execute Macro in Ms Access.